The Book of Wisdom

The Book of Wisdom

by Woo Myung

First Edition
published June 2014

Published by Cham Books
1202 Kifer Rd., Sunnyvale, CA 94086, U.S.A.
Tel: (408) 475-8783
contact@chambooks.com
www.chambooks.com

ISBN: 978-1-62593-022-4

Library of Congress Control Number: 2013948293

This book has been translated into English from the original Korean text.
Translated by members of the Maum Meditation Translation Team.

All creative work, illustrations, and calligraphy are copyrighted and
are by the author.

Book Design by Color of Dream
Manufactured in Seoul, South Korea

The Book of Wisdom

About the Author

Woo Myung, bestselling author of many books about Truth, attained enlightenment after deep introspection about life and existence. Once he became Truth, he dedicated his life to teaching others to become Truth and founded Maum Meditation.

His numerous books include *The Way to Become a Person in Heaven While Living, World Beyond World, Where You Become True Is the Place of Truth, Heaven's Formula for Saving the World, The Living Eternal World, Mind, Nature's Flow, and The Enlightened World* which have all been published in English. All of his books have been or are being translated into Japanese, Chinese, French, Italian, Spanish, Portuguese, German, and Swedish.

His book, *Where You Become True Is the Place of Truth,* was named the 2014 winner of the Eric Hoffer Award's Montaigne Medal, and the winner in the Philosophy category for the National Indie Excellence Awards.

In November 2012, *Stop Living in This Land, Go to the Everlasting World of Happiness, Live There Forever* was #1 on Amazon.com's bestseller list. In 2013, Woo Myung was the recipient of numerous awards for this book, including gold medals for the IPPY Awards and Living Now Book Awards. In the same year, he was also named a winner in various categories ranging from poetry to philosophy and spiritual for the International Book Awards and National Indie Excellence Awards, as well as being named a finalist for the e-book non-fiction category and Montaigne Medal from the Eric Hoffer Award. In the previous year, he was awarded three gold medals by the eLit Book Awards for the Spiritual/ Mind, Body & Spirit/Self-help categories.

In September 2002, in recognition of his efforts to promote peace, he was awarded the Mahatma Gandhi Peace Prize by the UN-NGO, International Association of Educators for World Peace (IAEWP) and was also appointed as a World Peace Ambassador by the same organization.

official website: www.woomyung.com

Contents

Preface

Part · 1   Truth · Enlightenment

Part · 6 Religion · Salvation

Part · 7 Poems of Enlightenment

Conclusion

Wisdom is to see and know the righteousness; it is to know Truth.

Preface

There are so many different books in the world, lining the shelves of bookstores everywhere. The reason there are so many is people lack wisdom.

Books about the end of the world seem to be popular but the end of the world is not something that will actually happen. The end of the world is living life with your consciousness tied to your self-centered perspective.

When one's narrow-minded individual thoughts change to the complete consciousness of the whole, it will be possible to understand what the *dawning of a new world* truly means. The world one lives in, here, will be heaven and paradise where everyone is truly alive; the new world is one where all people live as one.

The world has become a dark place; a place where everyone's minds are different and people live lost lives of pain and suffering. I write this book in the hopes that it will bring light to the fact that these sufferings and burdens are not Truth, and so that the world will become one where all people can be reborn as Truth and gain true freedom.

Life in this world is like a dream dreamt during the night. Just as you realize that a nightmare was just a dream only when you wake, from the perspective of God and Buddha, human life is a dream-like illusion.

I write these words because no one seems to realize that we become free from death and we live in everlasting heaven while we are alive when we are reborn as Truth, which created the great Universe, and we live as Truth.

We do not know when we are dreaming that we are in a dream. In the same way, a person who is trapped within himself does not know the will of the Universe that created and existed before the universe.

Absolute Truth is God and Buddha and there is no way to live without returning to its fold. Anyone can return to Truth when we know that we ourselves are to blame for all things and we cleanse our sins by repenting. I have the hope that all people will cleanse their minds and realize that the way to live eternally while we are living exists within ourselves.

December, 2003
Woo Myung

Part I

Truth · Enlightenment

Dō is not something that originally existed;
in fact life itself is *dō*.
However, it came to exist
because man made a self with which
he began to live. Therefore, *dō* is something that
everyone must practice, even though
it does not actually exist.

Some people believe that God does not exist. They want evidence of God's existence in order to believe otherwise. Is there any way to prove God exists?

E very moving thing is God. People do not believe this because it is not something that they can see, but the emptiness is God, as are all celestial bodies in the sky. They are God because they move. The Universe is also God.

The appearance and disappearance of the countless celestial bodies and creations in the Universe occur through the providence of God. People try to judge God's existence through their conceptions of what God's form and shape should be, so even as they are looking at God they do not realize it is God they see. This is why people deny God's existence.

The creation and movement of all things are done by God. If God did not exist, nothing would be able to exist. God is nature's flow so all things, just as they are, are God. People cannot see God because they seek God in the form of a human being. God cannot be seen with our physical eyes; God can only be seen with the mind's eyes. Therefore it is wrong to think of God with one's conceptions and then conclude that God does not exist. Before the coming of Truth, it was thought that only mind exists, but in the time after the coming of Truth, the existence of God will come to light. Such is what great enlightenment is.

God is things in existence just as they are, and all things with form are self-sufficient. That is, they have the power of self-existence. The innumerable stars in the sky are God, and they exist of and by themselves. We should realize that the celestial bodies run according to nature's flow by the power of God.

God is omnipotent and omniscient; God is also eternal and nature's flow. Man lives in suffering and he does not have eternal life because he does not live according to nature's flow. God is eternal, omnipotent and omniscient. God is all things in existence, just as they are.

If God did not exist, neither would the Universe and all creations in it. The power of God is expressed through nature's flow, and it is God who punishes those who betray the order of nature's flow: people receive the consequences of their actions when they treat nature in a way that is against nature's flow. Therefore, learning the order of nature is to learn the order of God; it angers God when one acts against nature's flow. The best way to find God is to stop seeking God in human form. It is wrong to seek God in a particular form for an ordinary person whose mind's eyes or inner eyes do not open.

Before the coming of Truth, God, when seen with the mind's eyes, existed in human forms. But now God exists as perfection itself; not in human forms but as real existences all living in the land of God. In this world there is no self, thus it is a place where everything runs as one, according to nature's flow. After the coming of Truth, God in all things will become one: the unification of heaven, earth, and man will become realized and heaven, earth, and man will become one. Everything is one because the real existence is something that exists, yet does not exist; it does not exist and yet it does. The Universe itself is God, and such is absolute Truth.

Where does human greed come from, and what is the standard that decides what is and is not greed?

H uman greed comes from the desire to survive. The desire for comfort and personal gain, which comes from having a *self*, gives rise to a person's greed. The standard for deciding what is and is not greed is the following: anything done for oneself is greed, whereas what is done for the benefit of others is not. From the position of Truth, anything done selflessly - when one does not have a self - is not greed, but all things done when one has a self is greed.

How can we be absolved of our sins?

When a person achieves enlightenment, all of his sins disappear. For this to happen, he must find his original self. People themselves make their karma, or sins, because of their human minds; in order to escape from their sins, they must become enlightened. When one achieves enlightenment, he becomes free of them all. This is the only way to receive absolution.

What is the virtue of yin?

The Universe consists of yin and yang. If everything that can be seen is yang, that which cannot be seen is yin. Yin is the body from which all things in the world are created. Although its activity is not visible, it is what created the universe and gives birth to all things.

Why do people need the virtue of yin? Yin is that which gives us birth and life and it is also what takes away our lives. Many people confuse something that was done by yin as having been done by yang. For example, when a murder is committed, people believe it was done by the murderer. While this is true, it is actually yin that caused the death, for death happens through the underlying force of yin.

The principle of yin is difficult for ordinary people to understand or describe. In any case, yin is also the administrator of happiness and misfortune. Although people believe that only what they can see is important, everything is driven by the virtue of yin, and it is what determines our happiness and misfortune. It is important to have a righteous mind and do righteous deeds because everything in the world is shaped in accordance with the virtue of yin. Therefore it follows that blessings come when one is upright and virtuous. Happiness comes when one is of a truthful mind; one must be of the true mind to be truly without any qualms.

Since the virtue of yin responds to that which is true and it does not respond to anything that is not, it is best to be upright and true, but it is even better to be beyond even those things: to act without self; to be without human minds; and to live as a true human being. Blessings cannot be found where there is pretence or falseness. One's life should be totally without falseness or blockages, and such a life is Truth. Truth is one; it is never-changing; and its origin is the virtue of yin. The creation of the virtue of yin is similar to one's body and mind being reflected in a mirror.

The reasons a person does not have a good life, namely the hardships in his life, are due to the qualms in his body and mind. This is Truth and it is the law of the world. Respecting and venerating one's ancestors is one of the virtues of yin, and one of the utmost virtues of yin is one's ancestors passing on to a good place after death. One of the gravest mistakes a person can make is to discriminate between life and death, and neglect and disdain his ancestors after they pass away. This is the virtue of yin.

What does 'of and by itself' mean?

'Of and by itself" means 'just as it is'. That something is 'just as it is' means that though its traits may change, what it essentially is does not actually change at all. That all creations in the world came forth of and by themselves means that they were and are always in existence just as they are. Because they 'just exist', they exist of and by themselves. It means existence and non-existence of form is one and the same.

What is 'nature's flow'?

'Nature's flow' means everything is based on and happens according to a certain order. Everything in the world took place, and is still taking place, according to nature's flow. Thus nature's flow, or universal order, is the work of the world; it is the work of heaven and earth. People try to fix and change this universal order, but each time they do so they encounter severe disasters and suffer. And when this happens they look to God, because they cannot overcome these disasters.

It is not by God that people live; they live by nature's flow. Teaching people about nature's flow is a big task. Teaching people the laws of heaven is called *chundo* (meaning the way to heaven) but nature's flow is something that must be taught to man and earth specifically. Nature's flow is to be within order; and to be within order is to be like water that flows; and to be like water that flows is to be without conflict and stagnation. To not stagnate is to be alive; and to be alive is to be able to always move forward. To be able to always move forward is to be able to arrive in the complete world. From the water's point of view, the complete world is like the ocean, which is without words, free, at peace, and without qualms. In the complete world, the conditions for life for all things are the same - there are no causes for dissatisfaction because all things are one. This is what it is to be complete.

People can also reach the *ocean* if they live according to nature's flow. Nature's flow is the utmost wisdom that people can have. One must try not to be at odds with nature's flow because if he is, he will eventually suffer some misfortune. Such is nature's flow.

What is *Chun-bu-kyung*? When and by whom was it written?

T he essence of the book, *Chun-bu-kyung*, is the idea that heaven, earth, and man will become one. In Korea, the philosophy of this idea passed down for many generations and it was eventually recorded in written form in the *Bae-dal-guk* and *Dan-gun* dynasties. The *Dan-gun* dynasty was able to last for such a long time because it was governed by this ideology, which venerated heaven with heaven, earth, and man united as one.

However, it is now a world where man will become the master. The work of man will be the work of heaven, and the work of heaven will be the work of man. It is a world where the work of man will be fulfilled in heaven. The difference between the *Dan-gun* philosophy and this new age is that the people of the *Dan-gun* era and philosophy tried to achieve their will in heaven, whereas now everything will be fulfilled here on earth. The *Dan-gun* philosophy was right for the people of that time, but the current philosophy - the age of man - is one that is appropriate for the present because it is in accordance with nature's flow.

The age of man is an era when man is of the highest; when all things are fulfilled according to man's will; and man becomes the center of heaven, earth, and man. The person who first received *Chun-bu-kyung* lived in Korea long before the *Dan-gun* era, but it was in the *Dan-gun* era that it was organized and applied to governance. Since the *Dan-gun* era, Koreans have guarded and held onto this philosophy throughout the ages and the passing of each dynasty.

How did Nam Sa-go, the author of *Kyuk-Am-Yu-Rok,* come to write this book?

Nam Sa-go is the author of book of prophecy, *Kyuk-Am-Yu-Rok.* He was a person who had *the ears of heaven;* he could hear messages from heaven. The book is the answers to questions about the future which he wrote down. After writing the book, he claimed that he received it from a god because he feared what might happen to him if he admitted that he wrote it himself.

God does not write books. Man is God, and God is man. It is not nature's flow for a person, a god, to physically come down from heaven, so it is not true that Nam Sa-go received the book from a god.

Kyuk-Am-Yu-Rok, a book of prophecy, describes the Savior as being the "king of the clouds in the sky", and "the true master of paradise". What does this description mean?

When it is said that the Savior is the "king of the clouds in the sky", it means he is the true master of the sky - heaven - itself. This is because the clouds themselves are the sky; the purple mist and the sunset are also the sky. Not only is the Savior who is to come the master of the sky, he is also the master of earth and man. He must have the power to unite heaven, earth, and man, and give them everlasting life.

Everlasting life refers to a life that is eternal. To be eternal is to be never-changing and the only thing that never changes is Truth. Truth is the energy of the origin, and in Korean it literally means "the energy of peace". The energy of the origin does not change; everlasting life is to live forever as the energy of the origin itself. The human body does not last, and such is Truth.

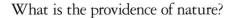

What is the providence of nature?

Nature, or great nature, is the Universe. The providence of the Universe is nature's flow. Nature's flow is free of obstacles and hindrances; it is fair; it exists and yet it does not. Things happening of and by themselves through nature's flow is the providence of great nature.

What is the origin?

M an and all creations in the world have an origin, and that origin is the same for all things. To be the same is to be one; it is not something that is here, there, or somewhere else. It is from this origin that we were born and it is where we will return. It is the place from whence all creations came, and where they will go back to. This origin is the energy or *life force* of the Universe, and this peaceful energy exists though it is without form. More exactly, the energy of the origin - the origin of Truth - neither exists nor does not exist - it is in between existence and non-existence.

It is the eternal, never-changing Truth; since everything came from it, realizing its eminence is what *dō* (Truth, the Way, or the practice of Truth) is. When seen with the mind's eyes, it is of a sticky but transparent form. The origin is the great true self.

Where does human come from?

We did not come from anywhere, and there is nowhere for us to return to. We came from the mind, and we return back to the mind. The mind is the energy of the origin which exists in both the states of vacuum and air in the Universe. This existence or substance is absolutely clear and yet sticky, and this mind is what created all creations and it is also what gathers everything back in. This mind has everything and is perfection.

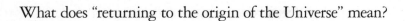

What does "returning to the origin of the Universe" mean?

Whether it be man, animals, plants, the celestial bodies in the sky, or Earth itself, everything returns to non-existence - the origin of the Universe. Non-existence is without form and immaterial, and it exists amidst nothingness as the original *body* that is the origin of the Universe.

To do *dō* (seek or practice Truth) is to return to this original body that is insubstantial and yet substantial, that exists amidst non-existence and does not exist amidst existence. The creations of the Universe, just as they exist, are this existence that is substantial and insubstantial. Therefore *dō* is knowing this existence that is our original selves, and this knowing is to return to the origin of the Universe.

Why is man called a 'small Universe' and is it right to call him this?

Man is called a small Universe because it is possible for man to have the Universe within him, as well as become the Universe.

While man's body is a small Universe that resembles Earth, man himself is not just a small Universe but the Universe itself. It is said that all creations exist just as they are inside man but this is only man's point of view. When man dies after having been born in the Universe, he returns to the Universe; likewise, the Universe exists, just as it is, in man. It is not man's thoughts that allow the Universe to exist. The Universe stays within man.

Man is not a small Universe but he is the Universe itself just as it is. Man's mind is the Universe.

In the Lotus Sutras, it is said that man's six senses - his eyes, ears, nose, tongue, body, and mind - will become clean if he diligently strives towards Truth. What does this mean?

To strive towards Truth is to walk a path towards one's original self. It is said that man's senses become clean when he does so because the more he goes towards Truth, the more he is able to shed human conceptions and fixed frames of mind. However, the state of things *just as they are* is the state where neither cleanliness nor dirtiness exists - where there is absolutely nothing. The word *clean* is used when people go towards Truth because their selves disappear. It is said that one becomes clean because his entire mind is eliminated. When everything is gone there is no self: only the original self remains.

What does the following poem mean?

The green mountain tells me to live silently,
and the blue sky asks me to live simply;
to let go of greed, and anger,
and to live, and leave the world,
as the water and wind do.

This poem was written by a Chinese monk, and it means that nature is man, and man is nature. Although it may seem in the poem that he knew that nature is him, he did not achieve full or absolute enlightenment. His enlightenment was only up to a certain level. He still had some *self* remaining because he was not able to see that he is one with the green mountain, the blue sky, the wind, and the water.

In other words, he tried to emulate nature which he thought was separate from himself, and he did not truly know that nature is him. Therefore it can be seen that he did not achieve full enlightenment. When one achieves absolute enlightenment he will know that all things, just as they are, are himself.

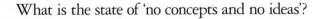

What is the state of 'no concepts and no ideas'?

The state of 'no concepts and no ideas' is to be without any thoughts whatsoever; when one is alive but has no *self* within his thoughts; when one is not bound to any ideas at all. Such is the complete state of 'no concepts and no ideas'.

It is a misconception that such a state can only be achieved or happen when one sits cross-legged with his eyes closed. This practice is only a means to go towards Truth and it is not the true state of 'no concepts and no ideas'. A true state of 'no concepts and no ideas' is when there is absolutely no self even while one moves, breathes, and lives his daily life.

What does the koan, "What is this?" mean?

This koan asks about the origin of the subject, whatever it happens to be - object, vegetable or animal. Man is originally complete as a man, and all creations (things that are in existence) are all complete in their individuality, but they all came from *me*. This *me* is the energy of the origin - the original body of the Universe.

The metaphysical real substance is the mind. Everything in the world was born from this mind. Mind, that is the metaphysical real substance, is man's real self, and this real self is the mother of all creations. Man is, in himself, a complete real substance as a man, but the place that this substance comes from and goes back to is the mind. If the subject of the koan, "What is this?" is a person, his complete or perfect self exists in the greatness of that mind. Therefore, the mind is mysterious and miraculous.

What does the phrase, "A mountain is a mountain, water is water", mean?

P eople see the mountain simply as a mountain and they see water simply as water. However the mountain and the water originally came from the same place and they do not exist separately. At the same time everything, just as it is, is Truth; namely, the mountain is a mountain, and water is water.

All things in creation, just as they are, are Truth, but man cannot see Truth. He is unable to find it, because he looks for it elsewhere. While the mountain is a mountain and water is water, the place where they come from and will go back to is the same, which is why it is expressed as, "a mountain is a mountain, water is water". It means that things, just as they exist, are Truth.

What is *Gesong?*

Gesong is a written expression of one's enlightenment. *Gesong* resides in the enlightenment, and the enlightenment resides in the *gesong*.

One can know by reading *gesong* whether or not the writer has been enlightened, because *gesong* is a writing from the heart. Only when it is written from the heart is it a true *gesong*; it cannot be called that when it is written from the knowledge of one's head. It is possible to know the place of a person's mind through his *gesong*, but usually it does not give enlightenment to ordinary people because people find them difficult to understand. The best or most well-written words are those that people can easily understand, therefore the best *gesong* is one that everyone can understand and gain enlightenment from.

What is the meaning of the Buddhist phrase, "Everything comes from the mind."?

Everything produced by the human mind is false because it is not Truth. The *mind* in the phrase "Everything comes from the mind", refers to the mind of the Universe. This mind is our Mother which created all things and brought forth all creations. Commonly people confuse the mind in this phrase as being their own minds, but it is speaking of the mind of the original self.

The mind of the original self is omnipotent and omniscient; everything in the world is made by this mind. It exists without form, and it exists amidst non-existence. When man sees this mind with his inner eyes or mind's eyes, it has a bluish hue and exists as a sticky substance. Thus it cannot be said that it exists, and neither can it be said that it does not exist. It is therefore Truth. This mind is the mother of all creations in the Universe, which is why in Buddhism it is said that "Everything comes from the mind".

What is the meaning of the phrase, "Only I am great in all of heaven and earth"?

The phrase, "Only I am great in all of heaven and earth", is speaking of the state when one does not dwell as a man even as he lives as a man, and when he does not dwell on earth even while he lives on earth; it is speaking of when one exists in the place of Truth, the Universe, where neither man nor earth exists.

This and *that* exist only when one's self exists; when one does not exist, neither does this nor that. One's original self is the Universe, and because this Universe is one's self, the phrase means that only the Universe alone is great. Man cannot become one with this Universe that is his original self, because he has a self which he continuously asserts. He must eliminate this self if he is to become one with the Universe and become the state where "Only I am great in all of heaven and earth". When he does so, he who is the Universe both before he was born and after, is a great existence. This is the meaning behind this phrase.

What does "the words of the Universe" mean?

The universe is without end. The universe only speaks true words, so they are Truth. Because Truth is genuine, the words will come true. The universe tells Truth to humans, and the words of the universe come true for they are genuine. This is Truth. Truth has no exceptions, and it is as it is. Therefore, when one speaks the words of the universe, everything in the world will be accomplished; so the words of the universe are the greatest.

One who can see the universe is happy. Happiness comes true with the words of the universe, so there is nothing greater. For humans to be one with the words of the universe, first, there should not be any self, and heaven, man, and earth should become one. Second, although people live as humans, they should not be human and should know the flow of nature. Third, people should know that others, who are not me, are also me. This is why one should be thoughtful when speaking and should not cause harm to others. This is Truth.

If mind exists within pieces of stone and dirt, what are the boundaries or distinctions between those with and without mind, and how do we differentiate between them?

Everything with form in the world is mind, and everything without form in the world is also mind. Therefore, it is incorrect to say whether something has a mind or not; all creations in the world is mind. There are no boundaries or differentiation between them.

What is *dō* (the path, the way, or Truth) and why must we do *dō*?

The word *dō* refers to a path; a path that must be travelled. People do not know what *dō* is, in fact it is something that everyone does as they live their lives. *Dō* is the very life that one is living but people mistakenly believe that it exists somewhere else.

One is doing the true *dō* if he dwells in Truth as he lives his life. However, if his life is not Truth, the *dō* he is travelling is a false path. Thus, while everyone does *dō*, some are walking down a true path and some are walking down a false one. In order to walk down the proper path, one must become enlightened. Only then can he truly say that he is doing *dō*. *Dō* is not something that originally existed; in fact life itself is *dō*. However, it came to exist because man made a self with which he began to live. Therefore, *dō* is something that everyone must practice even though it does not actually exist; one cannot ever escape from his constant inner battles with his mind and sufferings if he does not. Moreover, he will not be able to enter into the eternal place of Truth, and his delusions and mental agonies will last forever. Therefore, man must do *dō* and escape from all delusions. *Dō* is to arrive or reach heaven. This is the one thing that man must achieve as a human being while he is alive.

Anyone can become heaven itself if he sheds his self or ego. When one has found the study and practice of this, he has found the true *dō*.

What does *becoming one* mean?

B ecoming one means that all that are real and false in the Universe become one; man and all things become one; heaven, earth, and man become one. If we limit the phrase to people, it would mean that everyone becomes one without separation between *you* and *me*. The great *dō* or great path is when heaven, earth, and man become one; when there is no *you* and *me*; when all things become one and complete. *Becoming one* speaks of the peaceful unity of all things.

What is enlightenment and how can we become enlightened?

Enlightenment is when one comes to know Truth. It is not simply knowing Truth in theory, but truly accepting it in one's heart. Enlightenment in one's heart is the discovery of one's real self - the discovery of the place of one's mind. This is the only Truth that exists in the world, and it is everlasting and never-changing.

Previously, it was extremely difficult to become enlightened because a master or teacher who truly attained and knew this state did not exist. Now, it is possible for anyone to become enlightened of their original nature within one week. It has become a world where anyone can become enlightened, without having to leave everything and meditate in isolation in the mountains.

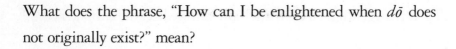

What does the phrase, "How can I be enlightened when *dō* does not originally exist?" mean?

Dō refers to a path to heaven. In other words, it is the path to discovering your true self. It is the path to the Universe. When it is said that *dō* does not exist, it means that life is *dō* and that there is no action that is not *dō*. People search for *dō* elsewhere but *dō* does not exist because life itself is *dō*. When one casts off all of one's self, he becomes the state of non-existence. This non-existence is one's original real self.

This original real self is the Universe, and thus everything in the world, just as they are, are all one's original real self. Such is the land of God and Buddha. Man lives in the land of God and Buddha, but because he lacks enlightenment he does not realize that he is living his life in the land of God and Buddha. Both sides of the hand are all *dō*.

What does, "asking the way while standing on the path" mean?

This means that even though one's life itself is Truth, man looks for Truth in the wrong places. Namely, it means that one searches for *dō* ignorant of the fact that when he becomes enlightened, the land of God and Buddha is the place where he is. Both sides of the hand are *dō*, and such is Truth.

Everything exists in his life, but man tries to seek answers to what he does not know from the outside. *Dō* is right where he is, not somewhere else.

What is the real self?

People understand that the existence with the original mind is the true self. The original mind is indeed the true self, but no one knows what this original mind is. The original mind is the mind that exists originally, and is the pure mind that does not change according to shapes. That pure mind cannot be said to exist or not; but it does not exist from the viewpoint of humans, whereas it exists from the viewpoint of Truth.

There is not anything such as knowledge, sight, hearing, arrogance, or good-naturedness within the true self. Even when the true self changes according to shapes, it is still the true self. Everything in the universe, regardless if it has a shape or not, is the real self.

People do not know the true self because they cannot discover it. There is nothing more valuable than finding the true self in one's life, but people cannot find it because they look for the true self that fits what they imagine to be the true self. This is not Truth.

How can one find the true self?

No one can see their true selves, because it is hidden by their forms and their lives. This is a similar state to a dirty mirror that should reflect back one's image, but does not.

In order to find one's true self, one must clean that dirty mirror. Namely, one must cleanse one's self. Cleansing one's self is to eliminate it completely, which is the way to truly find one's self.

Until now it was difficult to find one's true self no matter what kind of ascetic penance he practiced. Now it can be found easily by anyone. One's true self is Truth, and it is the Universe. Knowing that the Universe is one's self is the discovery of his true self.

How can people become enlightened?

E nlightenment is meeting the origin of the mind. However, it is no easy feat to get someone to understand that origin. In order to teach people where the origin of the mind is, one must bear in mind the following four key points:

First, get them to empty their minds.

Second, after they have eliminated even their selves, make them search for the mind.

Third, tell them what the mind is.

Fourth, teach them what the body of the mind is.

What is nirvana (spiritual death)?

Death refers to the end of a person's physical lifespan. However, if greed remains in his mind at the time of his death, this does not disappear, so in terms of *dō*, nirvana or spiritual death is getting rid of man's mind (soul) and his *self* entirely.

The practice of nirvana is the practice of going to God's world, but it is done after one has become enlightened, that is, after one knows the place of the mind. It is the practice of getting rid of one's self completely - all of his conceptions and habits from his life as well as everything that exists - so that he can discover his real self.

Discarding does not mean disappearance; rather, it signifies the discovery of the whole. When something disappears, it does not really disappear: everything remains just as it is. Such is nirvana; it is great enlightenment.

How can one reach nirvana or spiritual death?

Nirvana or spiritual death is to eliminate absolutely everything. In other words, it is to eliminate one's self completely. The way to teach people nirvana is the following: First, get them to repent their sins and karma, and their whole lives in order to eliminate their selves. Second, let them know when they are not repenting. Third, get them to eliminate everything and enter into nirvana. Fourth, make them disappear completely so that they may go to the land of God.

The teacher must actively get people to eliminate the roots of their mind, point out the self that must be discarded, and guide them towards heaven.

What kind of a person does the word sage or *dō-in* refer to?

People try to become sages by gaining enlightenment about something, but a complete sage is a person without any greed. Therefore, it is extremely difficult to become a sage if one is not walking down the right path or *dō*. It is easy to misunderstand that a person who speaks of extraordinary things is a sage, when actually he is a person who is possessed.

A true sage must not only clearly know Truth, he must be Truth itself. In order for man to become a sage, he must have a master or teacher; without a master there is no knowing how long it will take, if it is even possible. Not all sages are of the same level. A sage of the highest level is a person who does not dwell in life even as he lives; he who does not have any of his own individual mind. Everything exists amidst nothing, and while everything exists, the mind of self does not exist. People practiced in a cave or in the mountains because they did not know the true *dō* or path, but it is difficult to become enlightened in this way. In fact, no one has ever done so. The fastest way to become a sage is to find a proper master.

What are the *eyes and ears of heaven*? And what do *the legs of God, the ability to know other people's minds, the ability to become absolute nothingness* and *the ability to know other people's fates* refer to?

The *eyes of heaven* refers to the eyes of the origin which is the body of one mind. The energy of the origin is beyond time and space, and there is no differentiation between heaven and earth, so a person who has *the eyes of heaven* is able to see any place at any time. Only a person who has achieved complete enlightenment - a person who is completely without self - have this ability. The *ears of heaven* refers to the ability to hear the words of heaven - the words of the Universe - once he has become the Universe. Words from the Universe are absolutely correct because they are Truth, but it may not always seem that way because they will not always be consistent with the ordinary world that people's minds have made. When a person has the *ears of heaven*, he is able to hear heaven's answers to any questions he asks about Truth. When one has the *eyes and ears of heaven* as well as *the ability to become absolute nothingness*, he will gain the other abilities mentioned above as well.

The *legs of God* refers to the ability to command anything in the present world to happen. It refers to the origin's energy of non-existence, which is able to do anything. This ability is not attainable by ordinary people; only a great sage can have it. It is a truly awesome power to have, for one can make something happen by ordering or commanding the gods of a particular area. When one has the *power of the legs of God* the gods of that area make happen what he wishes for, when he does so with a sincere and truthful heart. The ability to *know other people's minds* is a knowing that happens when one has absolutely no self. Such a state, or such a mind, is non-existence, but because there is existence amidst non-existence, it is Truth. There is no way to know the mind of a person who has no minds; one can only know the mind of a person who has minds. This is similar to how one can know how much dirt exists in water, when there is dirt mixed into the clean water.

The ability to become absolute nothingness means Truth. It is the state of complete liberation, when all of one's self has been discarded. It is the state of complete non-existence; there is absolutely nothing but yet absolutely everything exists amidst nothingness. That is, all creations exist and yet they are non-existence. It is non-existence that gives birth to creations and such is Truth. The ability to know other people's fate by reading their minds is possible because the mind has no past, future, or present.

Are there many levels of heaven?

People have made different levels of heavens in heaven, but originally these levels of heaven did not exist. Heaven was divided into different levels in the time before the coming of Truth but in the time after the coming of Truth, there is only one heaven. It is man that divided heaven, but in reality, there are no levels in heaven. Heaven is heaven, just as it is, and there is only one. One is not Truth if he does not know there is only one heaven, even when he knows that there is only one Universe.

There are no levels to Truth; things just as they are, are Truth and Truth is one. Therefore, there are no levels of heaven. What is commonly referred to as the *ninth heaven* refers to the sky at a height nine times the length of the diameter of the Earth, and similarly, the *thirty-third heaven* is the sky at a height thirty-three times the length of the Earth's diameter. However, the Universe is many billions of times bigger than these lengths. It is without end.

Who are divine beings?

A divine being is a person who is completely without self. To be without self means that he has no body and mind. When it is said that a person has no body and mind, it means that although he exists, he has cleansed himself and achieved full enlightenment. Therefore, he has absolutely no self. Such a person is a divine being.

Because a divine being has no self, he knows all the things of heaven, earth, and man. He can freely move between heaven and earth. While there were no true divine beings until now, there will be many divine beings in the future. However, ordinary people will not be able to recognize them even when they see them because only a sage can see and recognize a divine being.

What is the world of divine beings?

The world of divine beings refers to the energy of the origin. A divine being is a person who lives on earth with the body of a human being but at the same time, lives in the world of divine beings. In other words, he is a person who lives in heaven and at the same time lives on earth. Living simultaneously in heaven and earth is referred to as the world of divine beings, but people mistakenly believe that living in the world of divine beings is to live in heaven with a human body.

This state can only be reached by attaining the absolute Truth, and only a person who has absolutely no self and has become the original self can live in the world of divine beings.

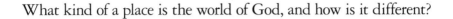

What kind of a place is the world of God, and how is it different?

A god is an existence that dwells in heaven. Heaven is a place that is different from the human world. The gods that dwell in heaven are the highest of all souls, and these gods have absolute freedom so they are not bound or restricted by anything. In order for someone to go to the world of God after he dies, he must achieve complete nirvana or spiritual death and have nothing remaining. It takes thousands of years for an ordinary person who dies with his soul remaining to get to this world, so he must be enlightened in his lifetime.

In the era before the coming of Truth, there were many, many gods in heaven. They had different roles depending on what kind of gods they were.

Among all the different types of gods, there is the highest God who is the lord and master of heaven and earth. This God is the highest God in heaven who governs the entire Universe and is omnipresent. Then, there are gods who assist the highest God; gods of different areas of heaven; gods of different countries;

gods of the seas; gods of the mountains; and gods of different districts. These gods are the highest in the areas they govern, and they punish any man or soul who goes against nature's flow.

Nature's flow is the way of heaven and Truth. Because gods know nature's flow, they do not forgive anything that is against this order. Such is the world of God. Below the world of God, there is the world of souls.

What do angels do in heaven and what do they look like?

Angels work in heaven and pass on messages from God to the Earth. They can be seen with the mind's eyes, and there are some with wings and some without wings. Those without wings are slightly more enlightened than those with wings.

Angels are in between the levels of gods and souls, and they become gods after a long period of time. They all have different roles and responsibilities, and they work in the area that they are responsible for. Simply put, they are the errand runners of heaven; they pass on news from heaven to people.

Angels have an especially close relationship with man, because they work on man's side. Although people cannot see angels, angels can see people and help them. They are often involved in matters of the world but they frequently make mistakes because they have yet to give up their own minds; their minds are not too different from those of people. Therefore, they are often scolded in heaven. Angels can find their true selves only when they pass from the state of being souls to being gods.

That end is reached through a long hard road of continuous mistakes and errors. Angels find it difficult to let go of the way they were when they lived on earth and consequently, they hold on to this for a long time.

Angels carry out errands for people by the order of heaven, and through these errands they often touch people's hearts greatly. Touching people's hearts is a special type of miracle that is a part of the job they do. People who have especially clear inner or mind's eyes are able to see angels and observe their work.

Dragons and phoenixes are thought to be imaginary. Do they actually exist?

Why would dragons be called dragons if they did not exist? Dragons do actually exist but they are believed to be imaginary because they rarely appear in front of people. They live deep in the mountains, and they move around at night by flying. There are some dragons in Korea, but only a very few. They live in Mount *Jiri* and Mount *Taebaek*. They do not have any wings, but they are able to fly using their scales. In Korea, the saying, "A dragon has been born in a stream" is used to denote a rare occurrence, and this saying comes from the fact that they breed very rarely. They hibernate underground during the winter and feed on reptiles.

There is another saying, "A dragon is ascending to heaven", but there is no place for dragons to live in heaven. They are simply moving from one place to another by flying. In the olden days, people did not know this so when they saw a dragon flying they thought that it was going to heaven. There are as many dragons in the world now as in the past. They used to appear in front of people in villages, but they have stopped doing so.

The saying, "pulling out a dragon" comes from great sages who would pull out a dragon of fantasy, that is, they would pull out the spirit of a dragon and use it.

Chinese phoenixes also exist. They live in China and they are as tall as a large person. They live in the mountains but are believed to be rare as they are seldom seen and are very few in number.

What is a guardian god?

A guardian god, sometimes referred to as a guardian angel, is a god that protects a person. Everyone has a guardian god but they differ from person to person depending on their size. That is, the type of guardian god that one gets is decided on by the size of his mind. The power of the guardian god of a person who has achieved full enlightenment is substantial, and heaven itself is the guardian god of a person who is absolutely without self. Such a person cannot come to any harm. Such is what a guardian god is.

It is said the time after the coming of Truth is an era when women will hold influence and power. What is the reason for this?

Women, or the female, represent greatness. Of yin and yang, women represent yin. It is women, or yin, that give birth to people and it is the female that governs everything in the world. Therefore yin is greatness. The origin of the earth is yin; it is yin that produces yang, which in turn creates all of creation. Therefore the origin of all things is yin.

The real world exists amidst nothingness. The nothingness is yin, and the real world is yang. Temperature, humidity, and wind come from yang, which can again be split into yin and yang. Reproduction happens from the balance and harmony of yin and yang. It cannot happen with yin alone, nor with just yang; such is the principle of heaven and earth. However, it can be said that yin is the essence and yang the shell because the origin of the creation of all things is yin.

In the time before the coming of Truth, yin was suppressed by the strength of yang, but now it is the era of yin and all things will be fulfilled by yin. Yin and yang are the same, and yet in the era of yin, it is yin that holds the vested power, and yang is hidden behind yin.

Women are great. The time after the coming of Truth is one of women holding influence and power, and it is the time of women. Thus, men must look after women with love and affection. If they treat women arrogantly or try to order them around, they will lessen their own blessings. However, when women do not act in a womanly fashion, the consequences of their actions will fall on themselves. Such is also Truth.

All blessings dwell in humility, not in arrogance. Although there is no such thing as a *well-lived* life or a *poorly-lived* life, harmony must be of the first priority, and everyone must become one. Our lives are short, even when all of it is lived in harmony. If we use our minds to live only for ourselves, the effect of our wrongful lives will be visited on ourselves.

The role of women in the time before the coming of Truth was limited to taking care of the family and home, but in the time after Truth comes, everyone will share in femininity, become one and the atmosphere of co-existing together will become heightened. Therefore, the position of women will become higher but they will only be able to enjoy these blessings when they discard their arrogance, pride, and ego.

What is the union of heaven, earth, and man?

T he union of heaven, earth, and man refers to heaven, earth, and man becoming one, which can happen because they all come from the same origin. In order to become one, all three must achieve nirvana. This union will happen when all the gods in heaven become one, and earth and man also become one. In the future, the union will be fulfilled.

All people will become one, all gods and souls in heaven become the vitality of non-existence, and gods on earth go to heaven by becoming the vitality of non-existence also. When one dies, one goes to the original body of God by returning to the original foundation. Heaven, earth, and man will become one in the future. A Savior is one who can give spiritual death or nirvana to all things.

Before the coming of Truth there were many different gods in heaven, because all religions taught that one still exists after death. And because man remained after death, there came to be heaven, paradise, and hell. In the future, man will achieve spiritual death and become one, as will all the gods in heaven and earth. Through this, the union will happen. Before the coming of Truth, man had a self that was not Truth, and when he died his mind or soul remained. Therefore he could only get to the land of God many thousands of years later, after he became enlightened. In the future, heaven, earth, and man will unite, and everyone will become one and complete.

I am the master of all creations, because in the future all people will go to completeness after they die, as will all creations in the world. Heaven will no longer be like it was in the old days, when an incomplete heaven existed and there was separation between *you* and *me*. Those who have achieved spiritual death will be totally without self, and live forever in heaven as gods. These gods will have the same form as they had on earth; man will be of the highest in both heaven and earth. It will become the era of man; an era of respect for man.

People's minds will become benevolent and good, and everyone will be one. Thus it will be a state of completion without conflict. People will live according to nature's flow, and wish for things to happen according to this order, and consequently there will be no greed at all, and the separation between *you* and *me* will disappear. In this way, what is fulfilled in heaven will also be fulfilled on earth. When the union of heaven, earth, and man happens, the earth will also be heaven. Therefore, people will live in heaven no matter where they are.

What is the difference between a holy saint and a complete person?

To be holy is to be without self. It is holy to sacrifice one's life for others, and it is also holy to live for others. Therefore, a holy saint refers to someone who lives for others.

A complete person is a person who is beyond sainthood. A complete person is, as the name suggests, a person who is complete. To be complete is to be completely without self. Such a person is at a level above that of a saint who sacrifices himself for others; he lives yet he does not, he does not exist even as he lives and breathes. Such is the state of a complete person.

A complete person has no obstacles or hindrances; he has no suffering; he has no joy or sorrow; and he is the master of all creations in the world. Therefore, he is higher than a saint. We will now be able to witness many complete people. For such people nothing is impossible because they are complete. It is the first time that complete people have been created, not just in the history of the world but in the history of the entire Universe.

Our future is bright because a complete person has appeared in the world; a person who knows how to sacrifice himself for the greater good instead of sacrificing blindly; a person who knows and possesses nature's flow.

What are the definitions of the end of the world and a new era?

T he end of the world refers to the time before the coming of a new era and it has already happened. The new era is a time when the way of heaven begins - the beginning of *dō* - and the end of the world refers to the end of the era of incompletion.

In the era of incompletion, heaven, earth, and man existed separately but the new era is a time when heaven, earth, and man become one. The new era has now begun.

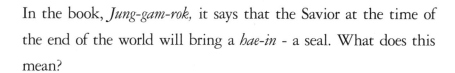

In the book, *Jung-gam-rok*, it says that the Savior at the time of the end of the world will bring a *hae-in* - a seal. What does this mean?

People think that the seal is an object, but it refers to the Truth of the Universe that the Savior will bring at the end of the world. In order to receive the seal, one must achieve spiritual death or nirvana and become one with the God of the Universe's original body. Therefore, the Savior must know the Truth of the Universe, be able to make people achieve spiritual death (nirvana) and make them become one with God. He is a true Savior only if he can give this seal to others.

The seal refers to Truth - which knows the principles of the Universe completely.

What kind of abilities should the Savior have?

He must have unfettered knowledge of Truth. He must be the king of heaven. He must be able to peaceably teach people. He must teach people about Truth. He must give them enlightenment and produce masters or teachers for the world. He must have a complete solution for people's lives. He must teach nature's flow that can guide man to find his origin. He must be able to guide man to fulfill his responsibilities. He must teach the ideology of the unity of heaven, earth, and man. He must have the ability to make all things happen according to the will of man.

He must give spiritual death or nirvana to everything in the world so that all individuals disappear and make everything one. He must make a world where only Truth exists. He must do all things without any false minds whatsoever, and have no conception of *you* as opposed to *me*. He must help people to shed their sins and karma.

Is there a reason God himself will come to the world as the Savior and right the wrongs of the human world?

This is Heavenly flow. The flow of Heaven means everything happens on its own without a purpose or a meaning. Yet, for the sake of giving a purpose or a meaning, it would be to lead humans to Truth by distinguishing what is true and what is false. People do not live as humans; religions are divided into many denominations creating illusionary worlds and planting falseness in people's mind.

Only when a person is righteous can he go to the world of God. In order to put an end to incompletion and teach completion, God will come and teach man the way to live in heaven while one is living, as well as after death. Such is the reason he will make a world where heaven, earth, and man is united. This is the will or reason behind God himself coming to the world as the Savior.

How will the new heaven be constructed and what are the new heaven and new earth?

The new heaven is a place where all people are equal,
where there is no human suffering whatsoever,
where man knows the honor of having lived as a human being,
and where one lives in a way a person should;
a place where all cultures and civilizations exist
as well as unimaginable beauty,
natural surroundings that are beyond imagination,
an unimaginable world of animals,
and where mythical creatures can also often be seen;
mountains and streams that are hundreds of times more
beautiful than those that exist in the world,
a place with access to all information,
a place without wealth or poverty,
where one can do whatever he wants for all eternity,
with nothing lacking for posterity,
and everlasting wealth and prosperity.

It is a place that has absolutely everything,

a place where the concept of *others* does not exist,

where everyone is one,

and where people live together with their ancestors;

a place where all houses are equal and beautiful beyond belief,

a place with only everlasting joy,

a place without enemies,

and where all things that one thinks of becomes fulfilled;

a place where all things are of a state

that man could not possibly achieve for all eternity,

a place where the space should remain the same though

all humans come for eternity,

and where there is exquisite beauty beyond imagination;

a place where there is no heartache,

only endless pleasure and beauty, yet no boredom;

a place that could not be added to or improved upon,

a place that has absolutely nothing lacking -

such is the place of heaven that is being made anew.

Part 2

Science · Universe

The center of the Universe is where
each individual creation is.
This is because the Universe is endless.

What is science?

Science is the actualization of imaginations and thoughts by using what exists in the world to make people's lives more comfortable. The science of the Universe is unfettered and without blockages because it is in accordance with nature's flow; because the Universe is omnipotent and omniscient each of its individual creations is perfection. On the other hand, human science, or the science of man, is made from greed which is not in accordance with nature's flow. Consequently, human science has created countless things that are problematic.

Human science is limited. Mankind will die by the very science that he has created unless a complete science enters the picture. Science is made through using that which exists in the world, but it can be dangerous when there is no understanding of nature's flow. Human science is fettered with blockages and cannot continue to make progress so its limitations are already set.

Those limitations have already come to light.

Finding answers for science from humans' knowledge is limited. The type of science that is produced without knowing the fundamental principles of the world cannot but meet road-blocks. Science has driven mankind's progress towards the most developed civilization there has ever been, but in the end only a complete science can produce real answers and solutions.

Human intellect and intelligence has limitations. However, there is nothing that the Universe cannot do because it is many millions of times more intelligent than man. Now it has become the age when man must become enlightened and practice the science of the Universe. In other words, science must be practiced after man has become the Universe. From now on, humans will be enlightened of the much deeper and wider science of the Universe from Heaven.

What does Einstein's theory of relativity tell us and is it in keeping with Truth?

E instein's theory of relativity is a scientific theory but even in terms of Truth it is correct.

The theory of relativity states that when an object disappears, it will produce heat and energy that is relative to its mass. People may have doubts about whether this is correct, but when an object disappears, it enters into the four-dimensional world that is perfection, so therefore his theory is right even from the viewpoint of Truth.

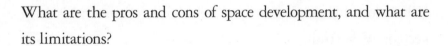

What are the pros and cons of space development, and what are its limitations?

S pace development has nearly reached its limits. This is because no matter how fast the object that man makes, it cannot travel faster than the speed of light. It is impossible to reach even a place that is only ten thousand light years away, because even if we could travel at the speed of light it would take ten thousand years to get there. Without new information, that is, without knowing the four-dimensional world that man is unable to understand, space development cannot help but be limited.

Aside from the moon, what we have been able to explore of space is still only a small portion of our own solar system. Completion or perfection must exist in order to explore this endless Universe. Space development with human intelligence has limitations.

Scientists claim that the Big Bang was the reason behind the creation of the Universe. Is this true?

S cientists have analyzed the Universe in their own fashion but they do not know the Universe itself. The Universe is without end and it is omnipotent and omniscient. It is from the Universe that everything comes into existence and then disappears. It is wrong to say that the Universe came into being from a big explosion. The Universe has always existed, and it is an eternal and perpetual existence. It just exists, and did not come about through an explosion; thinking of it in this way from the point of human conceptions is wrong.

The original body of the Universe is the emptiness, and it is this real substance that produces something into existence, which then disappears. It is because people do not understand this that they say the Universe twists, or is made. Truth does not change with the passage of time - it is eternal - so anything that is not in keeping with Truth is just a figment of people's imaginations.

Scientists have put forth a theory, known as the Big Crunch theory, that in the future after the Universe has come to the end of its lifespan, it could contract into one Big Hole singularity. What will happen to the Universe in the future?

Scientists' conjectures about whether or not the Universe has a lifespan are wrong. The Universe itself is life, so it is eternal. As such, it is the place of absolute emptiness, from which all creations are made and return to. The lifespan that man speaks of has an end, a limit, in time; time does not exist for the Universe; it just exists, as it is.

Man looks at this Universe from his own viewpoint and speaks of a lifespan, but this is because man's mind judges things to be the same as him. The Universe does not have a lifespan. In terms of Truth, if the Universe had a lifespan, there must be somewhere that it came from and which it will return to, but because there is nowhere that it came from or will go back to, it has no lifespan. The span of its life does not ever come to an end, so the Big Crunch theory is wrong.

The future of the Universe is to remain forever just as it is, with the repetition of the real substance coming into existence of form and then disappearing. There is no Truth other than this, and the Universe is something that neither expands nor contracts.

Is it correct to say that the Universe is expanding or that it will contract?

The Universe just exists as it is, but it is said to be expanding because people view it in this way.

Man thinks that it is expanding but it has always been just as it is. The Universe is just as it is, without end. It does not disappear, nor does it increase in size.

People cannot actually see the Universe but they speak of it as if they have, when in fact they saw it through scientific means. However, it is not something that can be seen. It is completely wrong to assume that its size can be ascertained by what we can see. The ends of the Universe cannot be reached even by light travelling for eternity. Such is what it is to be endless. It is said that the Universe is expanding and that it will contract, but the Universe neither expands nor contracts. The creation of things in existence also just happens. Such is Truth.

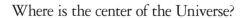

Where is the center of the Universe?

The center of the universe is where each individual creation is. This is because the Universe is endless.

How was the Earth created, what is its role, and how long is its lifespan? What is the reason that it is called "the star of stars"?

We may ask how and why the Earth was created, but it is correct to say that it was created and it is also correct to say that it came into existence of and by itself. From the viewpoint of Truth, the forms of celestial bodies came into being through the inhalation and exhalation of the great Universe. It is this omnipotent and omniscient Universe that also created Earth. The Earth will continue to exist for some hundreds of thousands of years.

When it comes to the end of its lifespan, the Earth will go to the four-dimensional world. Mankind will gain the wisdom to be able to move to another place before that time. The reason Earth is called the "star of stars" is because only Earth has the conditions to sustain life.

What is the sun composed of and what is its role? How long is its lifespan and is there another sun in the universe that is similar?

The sun is composed of a huge mass of gas. It was created for the Earth, and this is its role. Although there are many stars in the universe that are similar to the sun, only the Earth has living creatures and people living on it. The Earth is the reason for the sun's existence.

Its lifespan differs from that of other stars. This is because it exists for the Earth; it will disappear when the Earth disappears for it will no longer be needed. However, it will continue to exist for as long as the Earth exists. Such is the providence of heaven.

Why do the Earth and moon revolve and rotate and what is the source of this force?

The Universe used to be the state of emptiness, and from that emptiness the Earth, moon, Sun, and stars appeared. The Earth, moon, Sun, and stars are all completion itself, and they have the power to exist of and by themselves. This is the reason they rotate and revolve.

The strength of the celestial bodies to pull and be pulled also exists of and by itself. The ability of all things to live of and by themselves can be called basic, or original, instinct. From the perspective of completeness, the Earth, moon, Sun, and stars have no weight; they neither exist nor do not exist; they simply just exist as they are. Things that people think of as being mysterious are all done by this existence. It is by the will and life of self-existing God that the rotation and revolution of the Earth, moon, and stars happen.

Why are comets formed, what is their role in the Universe and how long do they last? Do they have fixed paths and times of co-existence or do they collide with other stars?

There are many comets in the Universe. They are made of gases, and move around the whole Universe rather than in one fixed area. It can be said that they are the brooms of the Universe, and their role is to clean the Universe. They do not have fixed paths and although they do collide with other stars on occasion, this happens rarely.

The way they are formed is similar to the way that other stars are formed. Some people say that comets are composed of ice, but they are composed of gases tinged with solid matter.

What is an intercalary or leap month and what kind of influence does it have on people?

An intercalary or leap month is the insertion of an extra month every three years, calculated by the length of the other months in the lunar calendar. As it is not a month that originally exists in the calendar, people believe that it is a month without restrictions where anything goes.

In the future, it will not matter what month, day or time it is, because everything will become one. To be one refers to the unity of heaven, earth, and man, at which time there will be no need to adhere to such things as leap months.

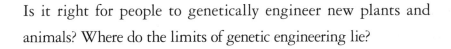

Is it right for people to genetically engineer new plants and animals? Where do the limits of genetic engineering lie?

It is not nature's flow for people to genetically engineer new plants and animals. However, it is alright to do so if they are needed by man. Man is of the highest, so whatever man needs is fine, regardless of its form or nature.

However, since such genetic engineering is not nature's flow, it will bring some big consequences and side-effects. Above all, taking care of what already exists is wisdom and nature's flow.

Scientists have been able to successfully clone a sheep using cell division. Was it right for them to do so, and where do the boundaries between the authority of God and of man lie?

G od's authority is nature's flow, which is what happens naturally, rather than being forced. God's authority is Truth. What man does is to make falseness that is not Truth; this is not right.

People do not understand that God is man, and man is God; it is not that the authority of God and man exist separately. When one lives and acts according to nature's flow, he is living according to God's will. Man is God, so he can only live without blockages when he is enlightened of this and lives as God. There will always be limitations to living when one lives according to human thought.

How true is the theory that man is evolved from apes?

The original essence of man and all creations in the world is that everything is just what it is. This means that a human being is a human being and an ape is an ape. A carp could not possibly become a dace because a dace is its own breed, as is the carp. Although they may look similar, a dace cannot become a carp.

Of course, some changes occur through the conditions of the environment, but the original essence of something is itself; a human being has always been a human being, it is not that an ape evolved into one. Many shapes of fishes are in the same way. A catfish and a snakehead, a loach and a snakehead are not the same, a crucian and a carp, and a dace and a crucian are not the same. In other words, they did not become different through evolution.

What causes the mutation of living organisms?

E very living organism has its own unique chromosome; man has man's chromosome, and plants have their own chromosome. Mutation occurs on rare occasions when the chromosomes of different organisms meet. While the mutation may make something larger, smaller, or change its shape, it does not change what it essentially is - its original nature.

Mutation is not caused by environmental factors. Mutation happens suddenly, not through long exposure to a certain environmental factor. When people or fish are affected by environmental pollution, such as curvature of the spine, it cannot be called mutation. When something mutates, its shape, size, and color may change, but what it essentially is does not.

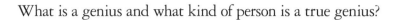

What is a genius and what kind of person is a true genius?

A genius is a person who is given a heavenly talent. A heavenly talent is one that comes from the Universe. What most people think of as being a genius is a person with shallow human knowledge, but this is not true genius.

A true genius should be a great master of Truth, not of falseness. A great master of Truth means a person who is equally at ease with both Truth and daily life. The type of person that most people think of as being a genius is someone who has a particularly developed portion of his brain. Such a person is merely talented and is not a genius because the talent or knowledge that he has is a human one. A true genius should have the mind of the Universe. When one is enlightened and becomes the Universe, he is able to become a true genius.

Are global warming and El Niño - the rising of temperatures in the eastern tropical pacific sea and the Pacific Ocean - the reasons behind climate change and extreme weather, or could sunspots be the cause?

E xtreme weather happened as frequently in the past as it does now, but it merely seems as though it has been happening more often in recent years because information now disseminates more quickly through the development of mass communication. Although it may look as though the Earth stays the same, northern and southern air streams cross over and change positions with the changing of the seasons. It is at these times that we experience heavy rainfall and snowstorms. When these become severe, they are called extreme weather or climate change, but this is not actually what this is.

Of course, mankind has harmed the environment and gone against nature's flow by polluting it, and having done so the consequences of such actions fall on mankind. For example, when the ozone layer is damaged the population will decrease until the ozone layer is recovered. This is nature's flow. Although it cannot be denied that changes in the environment which are precipitated by mankind happen, there is no need to be too fixated on whether things happen because of this or that.

Is there a way to make artificial rain, and which method is preferable for cloud seeding: dispersing silver iodide or dry ice?

D roughts are caused by people; that is, people are the cause of droughts because people pollute the environment which in turn causes the droughts to happen. People try to solve the problem of droughts by cloud seeding, which is not in accordance with nature's flow. Yet, it is financially demanding and hard to have enough amount of rain within a specific area. If it is absolutely necessary it is better to use dry ice.

The best way to have more rain is to reduce air pollution immediately. Air pollution has increased the amount of substances in the atmosphere, making it thicker, which is why it does not rain. Rain rituals, or prayers to God, can also make it rain. It also rains when people stop acting against nature's flow.

This means that while we must see and act according to things just as they are, we must not see existence as non-existence and non-existence as existence. This means we must follow nature's flow.

How do the wonders and mysteries of the human world happen?

There are many wonders and mysteries in all corners of the world. They occur, then disappear, not through the power of man but through the power of God, or the way to make them occur is taught to people by the world of God.

The complete world and the world of God is this place, here, and this world is the four-dimensional world. The world of God is a four-dimensional world that can change objects with form and weight from existence to non-existence, and from non-existence to existence. Everything is created and disappears through this principle but because people do not understand it, it is called the four-dimensional world.

What is the four-dimensional world, and where is it?

It is a world that is without time, space, and light. In other words, it is devoid of everything. It is an omnipotent and omniscient world, where the forms of all things exist but yet at the same time do not; where they do not exist and yet they do. Such is the four-dimensional world.

The whole Universe is the four-dimensional world. There is nowhere that is not the four-dimensional world but people do not realize this. All forms came from it, and when they disappear they return to it. Although everything of people's lives is the four-dimensional world, people do not know it because they cannot see the original nature of the four-dimensional world. It cannot be seen by human eyes; it is not visible although it exists. It is different from what people think; it is omnipotent and omniscient. That it is omnipotent and omniscient means that nothing is impossible. It is also perfection itself, and thus it is the mother of all creations. Such is the four-dimensional world. Dō, or the way to Truth, is knowing that the four-dimensional world is one's self.

How can people see and enter into the four-dimensional world?

The four-dimensional world is not a place that can be seen with human eyes; it is a world where there is absolutely nothing. Within nothingness, there exists the omnipotent and omniscient mother of all creations, so it is a world that man finds difficult to understand. In other words, it is difficult to understand because it is the original body of the Universe.

Man originally came from the four-dimensional world, and he is still in the four-dimensional world. However, he does not know that he is because of his body. The original body of the Universe that creates all creations within moments is the four-dimensional world.

Although people ask how they can enter into the four-dimensional world, they are already in it; they simply do not know that they are. Such is the four-dimensional world.

Why do materials disappear in the Devil's Triangle?

The Devil's Triangle or the Bermuda Triangle is located near the southern portion of America. It is where the Earth breathes, and the reason things disappear is that when the Earth inhales, objects transform into the energy of the origin and return back to their original birthplace. People find the disappearance of objects in the Devil's Triangle mysterious, but it is telling of the origin of the Universe that is the four-dimensional world.

That existing objects disappear means that which is real is non-existence, and non-existence is what is real. It means that non-existence and that which is real is the same, but man is unable to understand this. Thus, the Devil's Triangle will remain for man as an eternal mystery - a place of wonder. Only when one sees life and death and existence and non-existence to be the same, will the mystery be solved. People think that it is mysterious that a small ship disappears, but the Universe can make objects that are several millions of times larger than a ship disappear within moments.

Which principles formed the basis of the pyramids' construction, and what is the secret behind these principles?

The pyramids are the tombs of the ancient Egyptians. These tombs were built based on the providence of heaven. *Providence* means the laws or the ways of heaven, and these ways are speaking of heaven itself.

Thus, it can be said that the pyramids are heaven itself. There is no aging or death in heaven, which is why corpses do not rot or change inside a pyramid.

If people lived in houses that were built based on the construction principles of pyramids, they would live healthier and longer lives. Pyramids are heaven itself, which means that the ancient people of those times had the wisdom to build constructions that take after heaven. That wisdom remains to this day in the form of pyramids.

There are no special secrets behind the building of pyramids. They are simply Egyptian tombs for people's corpses. They were built based on the principles of heaven that is the four-dimensional world. However, they are not the complete four-dimensional world; they are of an incomplete fourth dimension which is why corpses do not rot there. Although people may think that it is strange, a complete fourth dimension is when even these things disappear, and such is perfection. Namely, a complete fourth dimension is when things in existence completely disappear into non-existence.

Did the legendary continent of Atlantis exist, and if it did how developed was its civilization, and why did it disappear? And will it rise again in the time after the coming of Truth?

The legendary continent of Atlantis actually existed. It was a huge continent, and although its civilization was not as developed as it is now, it enjoyed a truly golden age of growth. The reason this continent suddenly disappeared is because the lands above and below sea-level changed positions due to the crustal movements of the Earth. It is nature's flow that land above sea-level will someday submerge beneath the sea, and land beneath the sea will come up above sea-level. The sea and land are one and the same, and through the movements of the Earth what was once sea became land, and what was land became the sea.

The continent of Atlantis enjoyed a rich culture, and due to abundant natural resources it had buildings and motor vehicles as advanced as the ones we have today. Just as there are the oceans and continents of the present day, they too had a continent, the disappearance of which became a legend. This is a fact. Perhaps not too far in the future, the continents that we are living on may also become a legend. The land and the sea have changed positions many times. In the time after the coming of Truth, what was once the continent of Atlantis may rise again, at which time there will be faint traces remaining of their civilization.

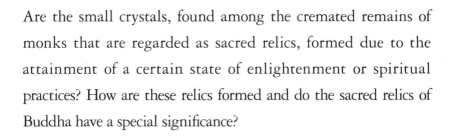

Are the small crystals, found among the cremated remains of monks that are regarded as sacred relics, formed due to the attainment of a certain state of enlightenment or spiritual practices? How are these relics formed and do the sacred relics of Buddha have a special significance?

People find it curious when something remains after a body is cremated, but these small crystals have no special significance. They are not always formed because the dead person had engaged in spiritual practices or attained a certain level of enlightenment; they are simply a phenomenon of bone-marrow liquid leaking. When there is an overflow of energy in the bones, this liquid spills out and solidifies into small crystals.

Although it leaks out as a transparent liquid, when it solidifies it becomes an extremely hard substance that does not melt even under extremely high temperatures. This phenomenon occurs more frequently in people who live alone. In those who have no self the color of these crystals are clearer and more transparent; and it is duller in those who have a self that they suppress.

The bone-marrow liquid of a person without self is transparent because the energy of his body flows more smoothly while in a person with self, the blocked energy flow makes it murkier. The small crystals are not a result of enlightenment or spiritual practices but rather a by-product of having suppressed the ego or self in order to attain a mental goal.

The difference between these small crystals and other gemstones is that these small crystals are solidified liquid from bone-marrow while gemstones are simply gemstones. In other words, they are all things that come from nature, so there is no real discrimination between what they are. They are simply what they are.

The reason Buddha had many such crystals in his cremated remains is that his energy flow was particularly vigorous, and he was entirely without self; his energy flowed properly and was particularly strong. Because he spent his entire life in spiritual practices, and he was a person without self, his crystals were very clear and transparent. This is the difference between his crystals and those of an ordinary person.

What is telepathy, and how can one's mind or thoughts be sent to others?

Telepathy is carried out by the mind, which is metaphysical. Telepathy is sent by the movement of a person's mind so only a person whose mind is empty is sensitive enough for telepathy. The reason telepathy can be sent is because human minds do not originally exist. Thus, when one's self does not exist, he can know another person's mind because their minds become the same.

Does an elixir or herb for eternal life exist in the world?

S uch an elixir or herb does not exist. It is nature's flow as well as being natural that people eventually die; an herb that stops aging and death does not exist. It is nature's flow that all creations with form in the world disappear. All religions that claim that one can live forever with this body are all false religions and cults. There can be no eternal life with this human body. Everything that people eat is in itself a sort of medicine. Taking oriental medicine supplies lacking nutrients to the body and acts only insofar as to cure illnesses and replenish strength.

Every material thing in the Universe has a lifespan. If people did not die, the world would become chaos. And because human life itself is suffering, if people lived for a longer period of time, there would be more people who would try to die. Although it is heaven's blessing that people have longer lifespans than many other living creatures, death is better than living for a long time with poverty, misery, and suffering. Even if one could live a long time in this way, it is not beneficial to him at all.

Part 3

Philosophy · Ideology

The origin of all creations and Truth is
the energy of the origin, which is the mother of all things.
It is from this origin that
all creations in the world came forth
and it is to this that they return.
When we know this origin,
all philosophical
questions can be solved.

What is philosophy?

Philosophy is the study of human life by examining it in detail. It can also be called the study of human thoughts and ideologies, but at times it only serves to confuse people because human thoughts and ideologies differ from Truth.

It is not possible to gain answers through philosophy no matter how much it is studied. The only way to gain real answers is to discover one's true self. Once this happens, one will know that philosophy is imperfect. Although there are some correct philosophical statements, they are lacking the fundamental essence; they do not answer the questions about human life and they cannot show us what perfection is.

Philosophy lays out human ideologies and thoughts. The problem lies in the fact that those ideologies and thoughts differ from person to person.

When one discovers his true self, it is possible to discern the rights and wrongs within philosophy, ideology, and human thoughts. Although philosophy is needed in people's lives, it is problematic in that it is not perfect.

One of the very first philosophers, Thales, claimed that the original substance of the world is water. Anaximander gave us the theory of "apeiron" (an indefinite matter that is infinite and indestructible) which tells us that movement of cold and hot temperatures creates fluids, which in turn becomes air, and from air all creations are made. What is the original substance of all creations and how was it created?

Thales' theory that the original substance of all things is water and Anaximander's theory that an indefinite principle that is infinite and indestructible is the original substance are not right. The original substance of all things is the pure energy of the origin.

Energy of the origin has no form but it is something that actually exists. Air is the combination of energy of the origin with other by-products so although Anaximander's theory is not right, it is close. In order for all creations to be formed, there must be pure energy of the origin. Energy of the origin is the energy of the Universe that exists in the entire Universe - in the states of both non-vacuum and pure vacuum.

The Greek philosopher, Democritus, contended that the original element of all creations is the motion and division of atoms. Is this right?

The contention of the Greek philosopher Democritus that the original element of all creations is the motion and division of atoms is not right. All things are created by vitality, which is similar to electrons that are smaller than atoms. This vitality is something that does not have real substance, but yet it does; when it changes into something with form, we call it creation. It does not happen through motion, but rather, through what exists as it is.

Plato said that there were three elements to life and man's existence: insight that comes from true wisdom, courage from will, and moderation of desires. He claimed that these three virtues are necessary for righteousness, which is in turn necessary for the greater good, which is the highest ideal. He stated that an ideal state is governed by a person who has these virtues. Is this right?

Insight, courage, and moderation do not realize human righteousness. True righteousness does not lie in these things. Righteousness does not exist in knowledge, courage, or moderation. True righteousness is when there is absolutely nothing.

A person who has no self is the most righteous. This is because he knows nature's flow when his self does not exist. Within the qualities of insight, courage, and moderation, there is always a self which prohibits him from seeing nature's flow. The ideal state is one that is governed by a person who knows how to rule according to nature's flow - by a person with absolutely no self.

Aristippus, a pupil of Socrates, became the first hedonist by claiming that pleasure is virtue and suffering is evil. What meaning is there in hedonism and where should we seek joy and pleasure?

This is simply Aristippus' thought. His view is twisted because he did not understand that joy and suffering are in fact the same. If man lives seeking fleeting pleasures, he is acting against nature's flow. Such pleasures are momentary and the after effects that follow are much greater than the pleasures themselves. The proper path is for man to live according to nature's flow, and not dwell within being a human even as one lives as a human being. It is not true joy to gain pleasure by acting in a way that suits human conceptions. This kind of pleasure is fleeting and it is not true life, thus one must deal with the consequences that follow which end with more suffering. In short, he will reap what he has sown.

Man should find joy and pleasure from within nature's flow. If one lives according to nature's flow, he will live like water - going along with the flow of things - so he will not suffer. The biggest joys, pleasures, and happiness all exist within a life of nature's flow. Hedonism is the pursuit of comfort and gratification of sensual desires but no matter how comfortable one is or how good his life is, if it is not in accordance with nature's flow, it is Truth that he will receive the consequences of such wrongful actions. The biggest joys come from living according to nature's flow.

Antisthenes, a pupil of Socrates, thought that true happiness comes from departing from interests in worldly matters and engaging in spiritual simplicity and honest labor, and that building character through discipline and acquiring good habits, being free from avarice, and suppressing oneself are actions of virtue which form the basis of happiness. Which of his points are right and which are wrong?

Antisthenes' thoughts on true happiness are reasonable but they are not correct because true happiness comes from being truly free of worries, but in order to be truly free of worries one must be completely without self. This means that one must live a life where one's self does not exist even though he is alive. When one lives in this way, everything becomes a source of happiness for suffering is something that does not originally exist. Penance and unhappiness exist because one's self exists; when one does not exist they will not exist. This state can only be reached by spiritually emptying one's mind entirely. This was very difficult for people to achieve in the past but now anyone can learn how to do so through *dō* - the way towards Truth.

It is nature's flow that man behaves in accordance with how things are; he eats when he wants to eat and sleeps when he wants to sleep. It is not nature's flow to forcedly suppress one's self. Personality cannot be built through restraining; it can only be found in pureness. Pureness is when one is completely without self, and when his mind inwardly is the same as his outward actions; it does not reside in the suppression of one's self.

The Roman philosopher Plotinus, who was one of the founders of religious philosophy, asserted the following: all things originate from the perfect virtue of the transcendent and absolute One. Although we can accept the One we can never fully understand it because it is beyond our conceptions. It is from this One that all things appeared like the emanation of light and all things are created and derived from this existence of One. The One is a transcendent existence so everything about it must be inferred from its derivatives. The first emanation is reason, logic, and thought and the second emanation is the soul, following which is the human body. Therefore, if our souls aspire towards reason and thought, it will ascend as goodness and as light. However if our souls choose the physical body and material possessions, it will descend into evil and darkness. Is his assertion correct?

When Plotinus said that all things are the One, he was merely guessing. This is because the One is neither good nor evil, but came from perfection that is the origin of all creations. It is called the One because there is only one such perfection.

It is also wrong to believe that when people's souls aspire towards reason and thought they will become goodness and light, and that they will descend into evil and darkness if they choose the physical body and material possessions. This is because these things have no relation to evil and darkness or to goodness and light. Originally, there is no good or evil in man; good and evil was something that man made by himself. Therefore, his theory is incorrect. Man himself decides what is good and evil and acts accordingly; good and evil do not originally exist.

Greek theologian Origen said that man and the whole world must seek salvation and that to do so is the process through which all creations return to God. He also said that complete people will come about through Jesus Christ who came to the world in human form. Life on earth is a continuation of training and discipline for people of the faith. Thus they must discard all desires, thoughts of marriage, military service, and government jobs and instead return to a unity with God. Which of his points are right and which are wrong?

What Origen asserted is not right because it is wrong to try and seek salvation from outside one's self. It is not through a particular person that one will find salvation; it happens when he completely eliminates himself.

Jesus Christ taught that heaven exists and that the kingdom of God is near but he was not the actual Savior. The Savior will save everything in the world and guide them to the land of God by making them eliminate themselves. Such a person is the true Savior.

It is also wrong to discard worldly things such as desires, marriage, military service, and government jobs. In people's lives, discarding is having. In other words, when a person does not marry, the desire to marry will take deep roots within his mind which makes it more difficult for him to go to the land of God. It is not through one's forced actions that he can get there. It is nature's flow that people do all that is required of them as they live.

Perfection exists when man does action. When man discards his human instincts, it only deepens the roots of his human mind, thereby making it impossible to go to the world of God. Such is incompletion and until now religion was incomplete.

Now, anyone can go to the land of God and anyone can become God. In the land of God, one lives life but nothing exists. That nothing exists means that one can enter the land of God when he has no greed at all.

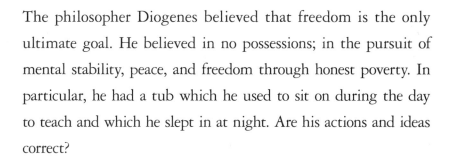

The philosopher Diogenes believed that freedom is the only ultimate goal. He believed in no possessions; in the pursuit of mental stability, peace, and freedom through honest poverty. In particular, he had a tub which he used to sit on during the day to teach and which he slept in at night. Are his actions and ideas correct?

There are things that people need in order to live, and there are many conditions that are necessary for daily life. The pursuit of stability, peace, and freedom through non-possession is a meaningless folly. Man should live with the material possessions he needs, but there should be no self in that life. It goes against the ways of the world to spout such folly and justify non-possessiveness.

True non-possessiveness is to have everything but to not reside or be in what one has; it is true non-possessiveness when such greed is completely gone.

The Italian scholar and philosopher, Bonaventure, said that theology is the way towards God and that there are three levels of theology: theologia symbolica (seeing God in His creations in nature), theologia propria (when we who have been made in God's image see God in our souls), and theologia mystica (directly experiencing and understanding God). Are his assertions correct?

The true meaning of theologia symbolica is that nature, just as it is, is God. Theologia propria is not to see God in our souls, but that our bodies themselves are God. Theologia mystica is not to directly experience and understand God, but that things just as they are, are God. God is omnipotent and omniscient so therefore all creations that exist without anything lacking is God, and non-existence itself is God's original body. Our individual souls (minds) are not God.

Nature just as it exists and all creations in the universe are all God, and God of perfection who enabled all things to exist is what brought forth creations amidst nothingness. This existence is what religions call the absolute. Bonaventure simply stated his own thoughts, and as such they are not correct.

Thomas Aquinas, a medieval scholar and philosopher, was canonized as a saint. In an ontological writing, he stated that there were five levels of existence depending on substance and form; first, the lowest level of existence that is merely a substance, second, plant life with nutritional souls and animal life with sensory souls, third, human beings who have souls with reason, fourth, angels who have pure souls, and fifth, Gods who are of an absolute form. Can existences be divided into these categories?

Thomas Aquinas split existences into categories because he did not know the original nature of things. It has no hierarchy; it is oneness that has no differences in form and shape. He divided existences according to his thoughts because he did not know Truth. The answer is this: the original nature of all existences is originally one. Each individual being within this oneness are all perfection because their traits are the same. Man does not know that all creations exist as oneness without discrimination and have the same traits. One should know that this trait is each individual's perfection.

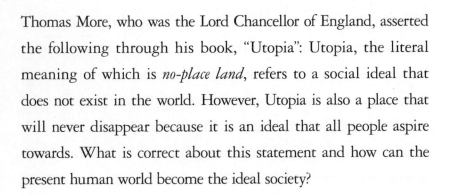

Thomas More, who was the Lord Chancellor of England, asserted the following through his book, "Utopia": Utopia, the literal meaning of which is *no-place land*, refers to a social ideal that does not exist in the world. However, Utopia is also a place that will never disappear because it is an ideal that all people aspire towards. What is correct about this statement and how can the present human world become the ideal society?

The ideal world refers to the place of the origin. If asked where it can be found, the answer would be that it can be found where the real self is. It is wrong to speculate about such a place because the real self does not imagine, or have any thoughts whatsoever. In order for the human world to become an ideal world, all people must become of one mind and live according to nature's flow.

Machiavelli, a political philosopher, wrote the following in his book, "Il Principe": "Political power is at the center of social issues and all things can be solved with politics. Problems arise when there are conflicts between moral and political values. While most people believe that moral values should come first, political values should not be placed below moral values. Rather, moral values should be used as a means to achieve a political end. If the result is good, it does not matter in which way the end was reached, namely, the end justifies the means. A ruler who exercises political power is absolute and he deserves to be protected by the power of God." Is this opinion correct?

Machiavelli's "Il Principe" is a statement of his own philosophy; it is the philosophy of an incomplete time. Neither morals nor politics should be higher than the other; in a complete society, they should be the same. This is because politics do not exist in morality and morality does not exist in politics, thus, if they do not run parallel to each other, it will cause severe conflicts and problems in society.

It is not right that morals and politics exist separately. Society can only become sound when morals and politics unite. The morals of society are also a part of nature's flow. Thus it is nature's flow that everything should be in keeping with these morals and that they be adhered to. It is because people do not know what nature's flow is, that morals become controlled by power. When this happens, nothing is as it should be and there are huge after effects. Morals and politics should be one; it is nature's flow to govern in accordance with morals and only then can problems be avoided. If a ruler governs by going against nature's flow, the consequences fall on all the people; not only does this create great social problems, the citizens suffer enormously.

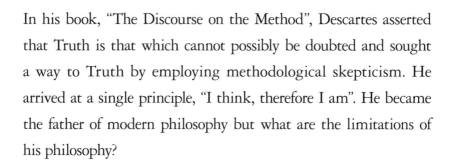

In his book, "The Discourse on the Method", Descartes asserted that Truth is that which cannot possibly be doubted and sought a way to Truth by employing methodological skepticism. He arrived at a single principle, "I think, therefore I am". He became the father of modern philosophy but what are the limitations of his philosophy?

The conception of "I think, therefore I am" is only Descartes' thought, because it does not mention what the source of thought is.

The conception that thought is existence may seem correct at first, but thought does not equal existence. Existence does not reside in thought; it is simply that which exists just as it is. Therefore, it is not right to say that one exists because he thinks. Man's existence does not reside in his thoughts. He is an existence that simply exists as he is. It is also the same for all creations.

Descartes claims that the interaction of the mind and body occurs in the pineal gland, which is situated at the back of the neck. Is this assertion right?

The pineal gland is not the connector between the mind and body. It is simply a channel, not a connector. The brain is connected to the whole body, not just through the pineal gland. It is simply a channel, a path to the body. Simply put, it is not that the pineal gland connects a separated brain and body; the entire path or channel itself is the connector. It is simply an organ that enables the mind to go to the body.

Spinoza, who lived in the Netherlands, never married and lived a simple life that transcended material possessions. Before he died at the age of forty-five, he asserted the following as a pantheist: existence is one, and it appears as the whole. It is mathematically one, but quantitatively it is the whole. This existence is nature, without which nothing can exist. If God exists, it must co-exist with the existence of the whole. Thus it can be said that existence is nature and at the same time, it is God. Many different forms exist in nature, but they are all various forms of one existence. God co-exists with the existence of the whole, and it exists as one. When God appears partially, it becomes an existence of form, but this existence has the substance of the one. Thus God is the real substance of existence, which is at the same time an individual existence. All intellectual content is the result of God's activity. God's attributes are in all things, but there are two that are only in man: thought and extension. Is his assertion correct?

S pinoza is correct. It was the one God that created all things in the world, but when they came to have form many gods came into existence that we know to be the creations of nature. Thus it is correct when he says that gods of individual existence existed.

God is originally one, but many gods came to exist because of the formations of individuals, but when these existences shed their egos, they will become one. Now, all things in the world have been made to become one, so while Spinoza's statement was correct in the past, it is not correct any longer. Now, only one God in which heaven, earth, and man have united exists. This is Truth in the time after the coming of Truth. Thus, while many gods exist, they are one.

Pascal, a French philosopher and genius, wrote his book "Pensees" or "Thoughts" after some mystical experiences of the Catholic faith. In it, he wrote that just as the things in nature follow given laws and principles, the spiritual world also has a spiritual order and law. Thus man's life should obey this spiritual order. Furthermore, a religious and theological order exists for spiritual order, which gives man's spiritual life meaning. What is right and wrong about what he wrote?

What Pascal wrote is simply the product of his mind from his spiritual viewpoint, but it is not Truth. Although people can see the world of souls through an out-of-body experience, what they see is a reflection of their own minds and it is not the actual world of souls that has a certain law. When people experience this through meditation or prayer, they call it a blessing from God, but it is just a product of their minds.

Therefore, it is imperative that we must not fall into falseness, and a study and practice to realize that the Universe is one's self is needed.

Pascal said that if a miracle had not happened, it would not have been a sin for him to be without faith, but it is a sin since it did happen. He also said that man is greater than the Universe because man can think of the Universe while the Universe cannot think of man, and that a small insect can stop the thoughts of a great philosopher. Which of these statements is correct?

T he reason Pascal sought to know Truth through miracles is that he did not know true Truth. True Truth does not exist in miracles; it is one and unchanging. He said that faith lay in miracles because he did not know Truth, and it is even more incorrect to say that man is greater than the Universe. The Universe is perfection: it creates all things and gathers them back in, and it is what makes the celestial bodies move of and by themselves, according to nature's flow.

Pascal tried to make the Universe fit his small thoughts, but there is nothing that the Universe does not know because it is omnipotent and omniscient; it is an existence that has everything. His thoughts are not Truth; they are one-sided and thus he cannot call himself great. What is correct is his statement that a small insect can stop the thoughts of a great philosopher. This is because philosophers do not know Truth. Thus when they see an insect and the thought occurs that it is not Truth, they must change their way of thinking.

Leibniz claimed that the real substance of the Universe is not atoms but *monads* which are units of force or energy. He says that *monads* are the foundations of all entities, and that they are indivisible, simple and do not possess material or spatial characters. And unlike atoms, as metaphysical substances their fundamental application is *representations*. Due to the fact that they internally possess everything that exists externally, they can be related to the variety of outside forms despite their inherent simplicity, and the variety of those *representations* is the whole world. What is right and wrong about his claim?

H is theory that the real substance of the Universe is monads is right. As a metaphysical real substance, all material comes from this. It cannot be seen by human eyes; it can be seen only by the inner eyes, and yet everything that we see in the world is monads. Thus what he claims is correct.

Leibniz defined time and space in the following way: he said we see the monads' function of movement appearing as co-existence and separation as space, and that we see the continuous unfolding of monads' inherent characteristics as time. Thus, time and space is nothing other than the order of co-existent objects and the order of successive events. Which parts of his theory are right and which are wrong?

From the perspective of Truth, time and space does not exist. Man's life made time and space; thus where you are, is time and space. In other words, where man lives has time and space but they do not exist in the four-dimensional world. Therefore, what he said is not correct because they only exist in the human world.

If we were to explain this in another way, space is where monads have come to have form, and what exists in that space is time. Time and space do not exist for *original* monads. Moreover, co-existence and separation do not exist either. They simply exist as they are.

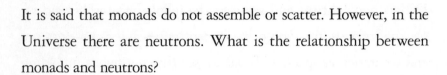

It is said that monads do not assemble or scatter. However, in the Universe there are neutrons. What is the relationship between monads and neutrons?

M onads are not something that exist or do not exist; it is simply an existence that exists just as it is. Monads do not exist where there are neutrons, and the real substance of everything that exists with form is a monad.

The reason monads do not exist where there are neutrons is that neutrons exist for the creation of monads with form. Because the role of neutrons is to help monads, monads do not dwell in neutrons; they exist of and by themselves. Their relationship is similar to that of lubrication oils and machines.

The philosophers of the European continent (Descartes, Spinoza, and Leibniz) asserted that philosophical knowledge and learning should be based on clear and indisputable foundations like mathematics and geometry. Comparatively, English philosophers asserted empiricism, and believed that the basis and methods of philosophical thought is in psychology and that awareness is a psychological process, and accuracy and validity of empiricism should become Truth. German philosopher Kant thought that logic is the absolute basis of philosophy and that all knowledge and Truth should follow logical thinking, and that the principles of logic should become the principles of awareness. Which of these three different schools of thought is right?

Philosophy is the study of the human world and the principles of the origin of man, but both academics and philosophy are not Truth, they are simply people's own thoughts. Descartes, Spinoza, and Leibniz's assertion that the basis of philosophy lies in mathematics and geometry is simply just their own thoughts. If philosophy is the study of the principles of the origin of the world and man, then all questions would be answered if they knew what the origin is. However, laying the basis of study in mathematics and geometry is far from the origin.

The English philosophers' basis for their philosophical thought is psychology; but psychology is the study of the consciousness and behaviors of living things. But the origin does not exist in the displays of consciousness and behaviors. It is not the answer to think that awareness is a psychological process, and that accuracy and validity must become Truth. If one knows the origin of the mind, it is possible to reach the objectives of philosophy.

The German philosopher Immanuel Kant believed that the absolute basis and methods of philosophy is logic, but logic is the study of the laws and formalities of right thinking. Therefore even if logic can find the original principle of philosophy, if there is no certainty it is not the original principle. Philosophy is the study of the origin, and thus all the questions in philosophy can only be answered when one knows the origin. The origin of man and all creations in the world is that which exists and does not exist; it is the metaphysical real substance that is the mind. The mind that is referred to here is the metaphysical real substance of both the states of air and vacuum in the Universe. This existence is the mother of all creations in the Universe.

The philosophers who believed in deism after the Age of Enlightenment or the Age of Reason, believed that God exists, and that he provided the laws of nature and the order of the world. They also believed that human life and the world move according to those laws and order and that God does not intervene in matters of human life. There is law and order and the world keeps going according to them. Prayers and paying of respect has no meaning; one only needs to live in accordance with that law and order. Such a God has no relationship whatsoever with people. Is this assertion correct?

G od is that which exists just as it is; God cannot be found in a certain or particular form. Although there is some logic behind the assertions of the English philosophers of the time, it is not right because they did not know they themselves are the Universe. They judged God according to their own thoughts which came from their observations that they and others have forms, but God does not exist in the way they thought. Man, just as he is, is God and has the power of self-existence. The discovery of one's original self is the way towards the one God, but not knowing that the true self is the Universe, they incorrectly asserted their thoughts based on form, relationships, and order.

Although gods are philosophical, the word *God* has a theological meaning, which is why Nietzsche claimed that, "God is dead". Is this statement correct?

The meaning behind Nietzsche's statement is that although God exists, people cannot see Him. There was always God in all things. This God is everything that moves, and in the time before the coming of Truth this was seen as the individual, thus there were many gods, but in the future all gods will unite and become one. It will become the time of the one God.

Nietzsche said that God is dead because people sought God from the outside world and did not know the true meaning of God. God exists but yet does not; does not exist and yet exists. God is the mind of existence, thus God is that which is as it is, and it is wrong to say that God is dead. It exists amidst nothingness, and it does not exist within existence. Such is God. All of these things becoming one according to nature's flow is God of the time after the coming of Truth.

Christians believe in monotheism, but Greeks believed in polytheism, while Spinoza believed in pantheism. There are also atheists. Among all these different beliefs about God, which one is correct?

B efore the coming of Truth, there were many gods. These gods were not simply souls, but gods. In other words, a god is one who is without self, and the world of gods is a place where one has left the world of souls where people have selves or egos. The world of gods is divided into five different levels of gods but in the future, they will unite, because only when there is one God is it truly completion.

The many gods will become one, and that one will be changed into perfection. Though many different forms exist they do not exist, and though they do not exist they exist. This is the status of one God. In other words, it is the Universe and the original body of the Universe.

The original body of the Universe is the energy of the origin. God exists yet He does not, and He does not exist yet He does.

This existence itself is the original God, and though one might have form if he does not have a self, he is a part of this original God. Therefore, polytheism was correct during the time before the coming of Truth but in the era after the coming of Truth, monotheism is correct.

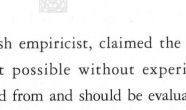

John Locke, an English empiricist, claimed the following: understanding is not possible without experience, and understanding is gained from and should be evaluated by the content and procedure of experience. All conceptions, which are products of understanding, are just products of experience. The notion of innate ideas or understanding is rejected. Understanding takes on meaning through the amount and nature of experience. Our minds are like blank slates, to be imprinted on by our experiences. If experiences become the origins of conceptions, the functions and processes of understanding automatically follows psychological effects, and the priority in philosophy should be to research and define the origin, relationship, value, and meaning of understanding. Which parts of his theory are right and which are wrong?

Not all understanding can be gained from experience. Understanding comes not from experiences, but from notions. Therefore the judgment of understanding must be achieved through notions and not through the content or procedure of experiences. This is because experience is not understanding, but notion is. That notion is understanding means that understanding is notion.

Ideas or reason are innate, but they cannot become understanding. This is because ideas and reason are both notions and the metaphysical real substance at the same time; it is through the power of the metaphysical real substance that understanding arises.

It is not right that understanding gains meaning from the amount and nature of experience. This is because understanding is not experience. Experience is not all that comprises understanding, but it is comprised from a portion of experiences, notions, and judgment. Therefore, the majority of understanding consists of something other than experience. It is also wrong that experience is the origin of conceptions. Experience is not the origin of conception - conceptions include experience and they do not just arise from experience. Understanding is knowledge that one accepts as true, but this is not from experience but it is a sort of basic instinct from what one acknowledges by the power of the original self. Therefore, experience is only a small part of understanding.

Rousseau, an Enlightenment philosopher from France, claimed the following: governments and lives where freedom for individuals and equality of men in society is protected should be made by all decisions in life being made through reason. Is this way of thinking correct?

I t is correct when Rousseau said that through reason, freedom for individuals and equality in society and government should be protected. However, it remains an idealistic and abstract notion because man does not know the origin of reason. Reason is a trait of the origin, and traits of the origin are nature's flow. An idealistic and abstract notion of reason that is spoken of in ignorance of nature's flow is not truly reason. Neither *your* nor *my* thoughts are reason; thus it is wrong to think of those thoughts as being reason.

Reason is perfection; as yet, no one has been able to speak accurately of the scope of reason because no one knew what reason was until now. Of course, these ideas from the Enlightenment era have aroused much interest and are in a way correct, but it is only when man knows the origin of reason and becomes one that authoritarianism will naturally disappear and ideals and equality in society and government will be achieved. Rousseau spoke of the foundations of human judgment, but he did not truly understand the origin of reason.

Hegel, a German philosopher, used the dialectic method of reasoning to study philosophy as well as applying it in every field of study. He held the method and function of dialogue and discussion as raising the level of knowledge of subject, object, spirituality, ideology, and history through contradictions and oppositions. Socrates also called the search for clear and believable conceptions and Truth through continuous dialogue *dialectical thinking*. Is the dialectic method correct?

The dialectic method that Hegel spoke of was a way to reach Truth, but it cannot be applied to human dialogue. This is because the origin is not something that can be found by opposing human thought; it is simply what it is. Thus it can cause confusion and mistakes. Although there has been much progress through the discussion of philosophy, the true origin cannot be found through the dialectic method.

The dialectic method seeks to find Truth by attaining a higher level of knowledge through the meeting of two opposing opinions, but this method is not the origin. This is because the origin is the place from whence objects themselves came; people try and fit it into their own ideas, which is why it is not right. When one knows the origin, subjects such as spiritual matters, ideology, and history do not pose any problems. But because man does not know the origin, man's thoughts dwell only in one area. That origin, which is Truth and the mother of all creations, is the energy of the origin. It is through this origin, that all things are made and to which all things return. All questions in philosophy will be resolved when one knows the origin.

Schopenhauer, a German philosopher, belonged to the pessimism school of thought. He thought that the real substance of the world of existence is will, and he believed that the power which controls the material world is also connected with the action of will. He claimed that the instincts to breed and the instinct of *survival of the fittest* come from the will to live, and that man's original nature is also the basic instinct to survive. Therefore, sexual desire is also a fundamental instinct to perpetuate the survival of one's species, and reason and knowledge are simply aides to this will of basic instinct. It is because of this that man engages in war and conquest and does not refrain from destroying life to ensure self-survival; it is the reason that the world is the worst that it can be. If we could choose, the best choice is to not be born. Therefore, suicide is acceptable. Man is going down a path of ever-growing evil, and the present world has no hope and the existence of God is no more than a false delusion. Is his opinion correct?

Schopenhauer's claim that the real substance of the world is will is wrong. The real substance of the world is mind. All living things just as they are are mind. He did not know that will exists within the mind. His claim that the power to control the material world is connected to will is also wrong; the place of will and power is the mind. His other claim that what maintains life is a basic instinct of life to breed and survive, and that man's original nature is also this basic survival instinct is also wrong. Man lives through the basic instinct of self-existence, not through will of basic instinct. Therefore, sexual desire also comes from self-existence, and maintaining species is not the only motivation.

Moreover, it is wrong to say that reason and knowledge are simply aides to the will of basic instinct. It would be more correct to say that reason and will are the aides of basic instinct of self-existence. Because man's life comes from the basic instinct of self-existence, when he is completely without self, he does not have any sins or karma. It is because his self or ego exists that he feels both evil and sins, but when he reaches the level where he is completely self-less, these issues will all be resolved.

Although it can be said that life is futile, one must know that there is absolutely no sin and karma in life. It is not that there is no hope in one's reality, but life itself is hope, so hope cannot be found when it is looked for too far from one's self. Moreover, the existence of God is not a fantastical one, but a real substance. This is because all creations, the world, and man exist because God exists; they would not exist if God did not exist.

Historians have largely categorized the history of the world as Antiquity, the Middle Ages, modern history and contemporary history. They explain that during Antiquity or ancient times, it was a period of nature and philosophy where logos ruled, while the Middle Ages was a period of God and man, controlled by providence and religion. Is it right to categorize it in this way?

Although historians can categorize and see the history of mankind in this way, it is not always right. This is because even during Antiquity, man worshipped God and feared the heavens. Man has had religion from the very beginning. Heaven is omnipotent and omniscient, and thus whenever it was necessary it produced saints like Jesus Christ and Shakyamuni so that man could know Truth and teach man that heaven is alive.

What is the difference between the theories of two Korean philosophers, Yi Hwang and Yi Yi, the former who believed in the theory that all things are two, and the latter who believed in the theory that all things are one?

From man's point of view, creation may seem to happen from the origin of two things, that is, from yin and yang but it is not so. The world exists because all creations came from the original emptiness which is the origin, and it is to this emptiness that they return. The origin is one, so from Truth's point of view, all things came from one.

The theories of these two Korean philosophers did not actually come from their own studies and research, but from the studies of a Chinese philosopher, which they then explained. However questions about Truth cannot be resolved through studies; one must actually know Truth. Truth is that which does not ever change, of which there is only one in the world, and that one is eternal and unchanging. Just as there is only one Truth, it is not that this and that exist in the world; all things that exist are energy, so the theory of one is correct.

There are opposing theories, one being that human nature is fundamentally good and the other being that human nature is fundamentally bad. Which is right?

Before all creations and man were born, it was the state of absolute nothingness. This emptiness of non-existence that is perfection transformed into man. This emptiness of non-existence is where originally nothing exists, in other words, where there is no thought, no meaning, and no existence or non-existence. Therefore, when one is born it is not that one's nature is fundamentally good or bad. It is neither good nor evil.

Truth is when the very conceptions of good and evil do not exist, but the reason that man has both good and evil in him is because he has the mind of self-existence.

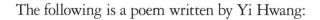

The following is a poem written by Yi Hwang:

Human nature is fundamentally good;
this has not changed in the past or present,
neither will it in the future.
Then how is it some become saints,
while I am just an ordinary person?
The reason is that what one knows is not clear.

Is this poem in keeping with Truth?

This poem of Yi Hwang is not in keeping with Truth. Human nature is not good or bad; so what he said is not true. His statement that the ordinary person's knowledge is "not clear" is right but who he saw as being saints were not truly saints. A saint is a saint only when he has entered the state of Truth and acts accordingly.

Is the saying that one must exercise self-restraint when one is alone correct?

This saying means that one should not think bad thoughts or do bad things even when one is alone, but it is not right. Not only does man have freedom of thought, but it is also difficult to draw the boundaries of what is and is not *bad*. People who were in the process of spiritual practice used this saying as a way to bring their minds to perfection, but this saying is not in keeping with the principles of the world. Man has good and bad thoughts and does deeds that are good and bad because he exists of and by himself. Trying to consciously remove these things will only result in a bigger mind remaining. Such pretentious actions are wrong. Man should know his duties as a human being, and live and act according to them, and the best way is to live without self, without suppression or restrictions. When one is suppressed, it begets more suppression, and when one thinks that one must not do something, it makes the desire to do it grow. When man is free from all suppression he can live as a true human being and see nature's flow.

What kind of people were Rajneesh and Krishnamurti?

R ajneesh and Krishnamurti were enlightened people; they had seen the state of absolute enlightenment but were not able to enter into it.

The state of absolute enlightenment is to be completely without self, and when this happens, the Universe becomes one's self. In any case, at the present time it is rare even to find people who know what the form of Truth is, so we must highly acknowledge even the level of enlightenment that these people reached.

Which aspects of capitalism, communism, and socialism are wrong?

D emocracy means that people conduct politics and form the society as the main body. Although citizens are at the center in democracy, it is not a complete form of government, so it has lots of defects. A capitalist system is advantageous for the wealthy, and those with money are able to become even wealthier albeit to the detriment of their morals and conscience. In this system there is no equality because of the wide gap between the rich and the poor. Although in the past people thought that a capitalist system was the best way, it will disappear in the near future because it is not a fair system.

Communism and socialism will also disappear because those who were governing the country in these systems were not just and exploited their people. It provided less for the people than those in a democracy, and although the ideals behind these systems were good they were not properly carried out.

It is now a time when ideology and philosophy will change

from being fettered with blockages to being liberated. In governance, all people should be equal; working must not be tedious or difficult, and should be set up so that anyone can work hard. There must be no hierarchy. Namely, there should not be a person above others exploiting them.

Proper governance should flow from top to bottom, from a person with a righteous mind. Therefore, there must be a plan for this to be carried out.

Part 4

Daily Life · Society · Ethics

The best way to become healthy is to depart from all things - to eliminate all the minds you have. When you do this, the energy channels in your body are able to flow smoothly. Illnesses are cured and disappear in the place where there is a complete absence of these minds. Therefore, living without human minds is the best for your health.

Is it basic instinct to be drawn to beautiful things, or is it because of one's feelings of inferiority which makes him continuously compare things to himself?

I t is basic human instinct. Man has a self-sufficient mind from birth - the mind of self-existence - which gives him, of and by himself, the desire to eat, drink, and procreate. He does not need to be told to do so; it is simply his basic instinct. This is the reason he is drawn to things that are pretty or beautiful. When something arises from a person's sense of inferiority, he craves and desires only that which he feels is lacking in himself, but basic instinct is the same for everyone - all people find good things to be good and bad things to be bad.

What is a person's *disposition* or *bent of mind*? How is it created, and why does it disappear when one becomes enlightened?

When a person has become the state where he has absolutely no self, he can see other people's dispositions; sometimes he can see other's dispositions are dark or murky. A person's disposition is located on either side of his chest, spreading downwards past his lower belly. If one's disposition is of a blackish hue, the person is greedy and desires for money, love or such.

The disposition is a manifestation of one's brain which is the mind. The disposition of a person who cleanses his mind is clear, and in order for even this to disappear, one must achieve absolute enlightenment - when there is no self at all. We commonly believe that if we live without human minds, we will lose everything. In fact, not only does everything remain as it is, we gain even more.

The disposition located on the left side of the body shows one's greed for money and the right side shows his greed for love. If those desires are not needed at the present time, they form a blackish mass and attach to the left and right side of his belly button. Ordinary people cannot see someone's disposition.

What are the roots of the human mind? Why do thoughts arise like clouds when the thoughts originally did not exist, and why do they not disappear but stay and become stronger and more stubborn?

T he roots of human minds are arrogance, pride, and greed which people find difficult to discard. The reason man cannot give up these minds is because they are tools that help to sustain his existence. It is said that the roots of the human mind are deep. This means that one's mind has become dark and thick because of his greed, and that this disposition has taken over a large part of his mind.

When a person is young, he does not have minds. They are made as he lives his life and they settle in his chest like a cloud. They continue to breed other minds, and in doing so they harden and become larger. The way to take off these minds is to repent but this cannot wholly remove them all, which is why one must liberate himself completely through *do* - by seeking Truth.

Why do we dream while we sleep?

A dream is a by-product of one's thoughts. A person's thoughts are his mind. How resolute you are when you make up your mind about something can vary; you can make up your mind in a *big* way or a *small* way. In the same way, there are two types of dreams: dreams about yourself, and dreams about the world of the true mind. We dream as expressions of our mind. Experiences during the day become thoughts, and the subconscious thoughts appear as dreams.

Dreams are the unconscious state of one's mind. That is, dreams are an expression of one's mind. When one's mind is self-centered, his dream is self-centered, and when one's dream is of the original mind, he becomes the original mind. When dreams are transferred to our memories, we remember them - that is, they remain. The reason we do not remember some dreams is we tend to forget dreams about the real self quickly.

What is the difference between ordinary dreams and *taemong*s, which are dreams of particular significance about the child dreamt during the pregnancy?

I nterpretations of dreams can be correct because dreams are an expression of a person's mind, but they are not always right. The reason expectant mothers dream *taemong*s is because a baby is a present or blessing from heaven, and the original self gives us certain signs about the child about to be born. It is possible to know the child's fate through the signs given in a *taemong*.

However, it is difficult for ordinary people to interpret *taemong*s. One can know a child's fate through *taemong*s because the real self is Truth and therefore, foresight by the real self is true.

What kind of a life is a *well-lived* life?

The way for a person to live well is to enter into nature's flow and behave like a true human being. It is no easy feat to completely eliminate one's self and live without it, but it can be said that a life that is lived without attachments to life is a truly *well-lived* life. All people have agonies, suffering, and heavy burdens in their lives, but when a person eliminates his self and does not bear those burdens, he is living a good life.

It is human to speak grand words but behave differently when he meets circumstances that demand sacrifice or encroach on him or his life. When one's self no longer exists, the conflicts in his life disappear and he is no longer attached to his life. This is a well-lived life.

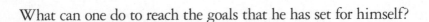

What can one do to reach the goals that he has set for himself?

A goal is a target. Above all, one must act in a way that is in accordance to the goals. The main reason people do not reach their goals is they lack action. Lacking action means that they are without movement, and movement is sacrifice. Sacrifice is gathering other's power.

To achieve a goal, one should use other's power. This power comes from his actions and sacrifices. It is possible to exceed one's goals when there is action, but without action, a goal can never be reached and remains as a dream.

The fundamental reason people are not able to reach their goals is they are without action and have a self; their bodies are too precious so they are unable to put in the action to reach their goals. In any case, the easiest way to reach a goal is through action.

After finishing their studies, young people look for work in order to make a living, as well as for self improvement and to contribute to society. How can one succeed after finding a job?

E veryone must have jobs in order to live and nowadays people prefer white-collar work to blue-collar work. People tend to blindly study and take accreditation or qualification exams in order to find a job, and while this is natural it is not without its share of drawbacks. The proper way to find employment is to first look for work that you enjoy. Second, look for work that you have an aptitude for. Third, there must be a guaranteed pay off. Still, it is not easy to find a job that suits all three elements. It is important to make a good decision at first, but you should not be bound to finding an ideal job. If it is difficult to find a job, one must be proactive rather than just wishing for an ideal job - keeping in mind that rather than trying to fit yourself to the job, you should become the job itself. You can succeed when you work with the mindset that you will become the best in that field - even though it may not be work that is acknowledged by other people.

People complain that there are not enough jobs, but in fact there are many. Regardless of the field you are in, if you become outstanding it is possible to succeed more quickly than people who have jobs that other people envy. Instead of just looking for the job you desire, do your best and become the best at what you do. To do this, the work must become your very self, and you must be without self. To be without self means you must be constant in your work. However, people find this difficult because the human mind is fickle and changes from moment to moment. Successful people are rare because most people try to succeed through shallow cunning and they do not work with this kind of constancy.

In order to be successful, one must be dedicated. Dedication means to devote your whole mind and body; it is to be without self and simply work. This is the way to succeed. It is easy to say that one's thoughts and actions must be the same, but people just think and do not act. They dig their own graves.

When a person has a humble attitude and works twice as hard as other people in order to have the same result, he can succeed. A person who complains that he is not being paid enough for the work cannot succeed. If one works so hard that he surprises other people, his sacrifice will move other people, and it is through the strength of other people that he will succeed.

What is *moderation?*

*M*oderation means that there is no overflow or anything
lacking. In terms of Truth, *moderation* means perfection
or completion that is in between existence and non-existence.
However *moderation* as commonly spoken of refers to human
philosophy and not Truth. It simply speaks of a peaceful way to
live human life, so there is nothing to be learned from this.

Moderation in Confucianism is the ideology of the unity of
heaven and man. No one truly knows how this unity will come
about. The unity of heaven and man means these two things
become one. Man comes from the emptiness of non-existence
and returns to it, so when his self completely disappears he
becomes vitality, which is the emptiness of non-existence. This
is the unity of heaven and man. The ideas and thoughts of a
person who has not achieved this unity is not Truth. Truth does
not reside in what one knows - everything that exists, just as it
is, is Truth.

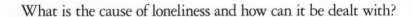

What is the cause of loneliness and how can it be dealt with?

L oneliness takes many forms. A person can feel lonely when he is alone or feels neglected, but there is also the loneliness that he himself makes. Loneliness is felt because one's self exists. When he - the self - does not exist, he does not feel lonely.

All people live lonely lives. It is fine to console oneself by thinking of those who are worse off than himself. Loneliness is made by one's self; that is, it is not something that originally exists. It is possible to lose oneself in the thought that he is lonely or neglected. All people live such lives so it is important not to further make the non-existent minds of loneliness.

Where should we seek joy and happiness?

Life is a continuous series of difficult times. But without any pleasure life becomes so dreary that one would wish for death. There is no meaning in human life. People find living life difficult because they live their lives without meaning.

However, one can live free of worries when he has absolutely no self. Living without worries is the ultimate blessing-the blessing of blessings. There is nothing to gain or have in life; everything is futile because physical or sensory pleasures are momentary and only bring more suffering. When one lives without self, unhappiness is no longer unhappiness. Nothing is one's self, so things as they are, are the utmost happiness. One's life, just as it is, is a happy and joyful one.

Knowing nature's flow and living accordingly is a joyful and happy life. One can be happy and joyful because nature's flow is mutual affection. Nature's flow exists in the place where one's self does not exist. Therefore the way of man is nature's flow. The way of man and the way of heaven is one and the same, so we must live according to nature's flow.

What is the purpose behind life and living?

M an is originally born from the original foundation, so to be born is to change from non-existence to existence. When man comes to have form, he begins to believe that he is his form and sets goals and objectives that are related or bound to his form. However, after one has eliminated himself, his goals and objectives are those of a saint-they are the way of Truth. These are the best goals - the best purpose-that one can have.

How should we educate our children?

The best way to raise our children is to teach them how to eliminate their selves. If this is difficult to teach, you should teach sacrifice to children. It is the way to success.

People try to reap a harvest without sowing seeds, but for such people their harvest will be one of weeds. Sacrifice is the true seed. The bigger the sacrifice, the better the seed it becomes. There is no way to grow a true plant unless you plant a true seed. If you teach your children to act only for their own benefit and to use their shallow cunning, rather than becoming a big tree they will become weak plants that are likely to die. They will not be able to grow properly and they will have many limitations.

Only when a person sacrifices with a truthful mind, can he gather other people's strength and become a big tree. Living this way is Truth but people live imprisoned by their small selves, which have deviated from their original mind. Sacrifice is the greatest driving force for one's life in society. It is the shortcut to success and it raises people's possibilities to infinity.

Is there any meaning in being by one's parent's deathbed?

Before a person departs his life, saying what is in your heart is a good way to resolve regrets and sorrow. In other words, it is good for children to be by their parent's deathbed because it helps to alleviate their parent's burden. When a person has many burdens in his mind when he dies, his attachments to this world remain and he must go through more suffering. Being by a person's deathbed helps to lessen the burdens of his mind. During this time, children should sit by their parents with a comfortable and peaceful mind rather than being distraught or crying.

Why must we venerate our ancestors?

Ancestors are all of our predecessors since the progenitors of mankind. We perform ancestral rites for the following reasons: first, we are not separate from our ancestors. Second, our ancestors' souls are unable to let go of the habits they had as human beings and they look for food for a hundred years. Therefore, we must respect and venerate them by performing ancestral rites for our ancestors up to the fourth generation before us. Third, we must ensure they do not feel sad and neglected. Fourth, we must think that they are living with us. Fifth, we were born through their bodies, so we are actually living with them. Therefore, we must not sadden them. Sixth, we can receive the virtue of yin only when we venerate them. The virtue of yin is invisible, but we live by its strength. Often there are things that are impossible, no matter how hard one tries. We must have the virtue of yin if things are to work out smoothly. Therefore, we must venerate our ancestors.

The descendants of families who properly perform ancestral rites live good lives. One's ancestors are his own self, and he is his ancestors, so we must not neglect them. These are the reasons we must perform ancestral rites.

Every human being and every creation in the world have minds of individual beings. How can man, animate beings, and inanimate objects survive if they discard their individual minds?

True mind is the core and the origin of everything in the world. True mind exists but it does not; it does not exist but it exists. It is the existence as it is. However, people are ignorant and misunderstand; they think they cannot live without human mind. The original mind exists as it is no matter the human mind exists or not. Yet people have their own human mind, and think that individual mind is what constitutes theirselves.

When the original mind exists but one's human minds do not, he lives a true life. One's own individual mind only confines and restricts; it does not help him at all. Becoming free from one's ego entirely is *dō* or going towards Truth. Only when one lives with the original mind, is his life a well-lived life.

When one's own minds are added to this original mind, they form to make his soul and become the source of various delusions. When one's individual mind does not exist, he can live according to nature's flow - a complete life of Truth.

Why is man great?

Man's greatness comes from the fact that only man has the wisdom to reach heaven. Furthermore, only man has the ability to govern over all creations, but this must come after he discovers his true self.

In all other respects, man is not great. Man's greatness lies in living a life that is as it is - a life of Truth; a true life. However, if he has any attachment to that life, there is no greatness in his life.

How is health related to the mind?

People believe that a healthy mind resides in a healthy body, but they are wrong. Only when a mind is healthy can a body become healthy. This means the body is less susceptible to illnesses. A mind becomes healthy when there is no possession in the mind, which means there is no self. This is the best way to be healthy.

Physical exercise frees one's diseased body from agony and delusions, and gives a sense of achievement through movement. Exercise does help physical health, but to maintain health with exercise, people have to be very diligent. People who work hard are healthy because they do not have time to plant disease in their mind. Although exercise keeps a body healthy, when people stop exercising, they will be even more exposed to disease. We cannot say which exercise is the best because every exercise has pros and cons.

Naturally, people who move a lot live longer, but the best way to be healthy is to leave everything behind. There is no better way to be healthy than getting rid of mind. When there is no mind within the true mind, energy and bloods circulate smoothly and cure every disease in the midst of the empty mind. Thus, to live without mind is the best way to be healthy.

What are the differences between Western and Eastern medicine, and what are their pros and cons?

E astern medicine derives from the study of the original body of the Universe. Western medicine focuses on treating the affected area itself. Western and Eastern medicine have their respective strengths and weaknesses. Eastern medicine treats the fundamental or underlying causes, while Western medicine treats the affected area or symptoms. It is not possible to say one is better than the other. All human illnesses come from the mind; one's mind is the most fundamental cause of illness. Therefore if one's mind does not change, he will remain sick.

Illnesses do not originally exist. The reason people, of all creations in the world, have the most illnesses is because people each have their own individual minds and these minds cause illnesses. Illnesses do not exist in the place where one's own mind does not exist. Illnesses were not made by someone, nor are they punishments from heaven. They are made by one's self. Whether one uses Western or Eastern medicine or both, treatments are more effective if one accepts the treatment in his mind. For example, it is better to treat a broken leg with Western medicine, while it is better to treat an illness that has taken root deep inside the body with Eastern medicine.

However, a better way than either of these is to become the state where one absolutely does not exist; the state where one no longer fears death. All animals, plants, and inanimate creatures dislike themselves disappearing. Illnesses exist because of the unwillingness to let go of existence, but when we do let go illnesses disappear within moments. For example, even when someone is very ill he will steadily become better if he accepts death and gains peace of mind, as if the illness had only existed in his mind.

If all illnesses come from the mind, through which channels are minds transferred to the areas of the body, and in which areas of the body do illnesses settle, take root, and grow?

When it is said that illnesses come from the mind, it means that a person becomes ill when he is not of the rightful mind. Not being of the rightful mind means that he is different on the outside than he is on the inside and his thoughts remaining in his subconscious mind are delivered to each area of the body through the nervous system. When this happens they hinder blood circulation, which causes various illnesses. A person's mind resides in the middle of his brain, and his minds are delivered to each area of his body.

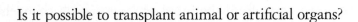

Is it possible to transplant animal or artificial organs?

An organ transplant should be done between humans. Although the transplantation of artificial organs happens when absolutely necessary, it has limitations. Animal organs do not fit to human bodies. An animal body and a human body would be out of balance, and even though organs are transplanted, they will not function after a short period of time because humans and animals have different chromosomes.

Is it against nature's flow to conceive a child through in-vitro fertilization?

B abies should be born through a couple's physical relations; it is against the ways of heaven to take another person's sperm and make a baby through insemination. Therefore, the consequences of such actions will fall on the person who wanted the procedure to be done. Moreover, these means are against the rules of original people, and the nature of a child born through such means will be different from other children. Sometimes, the baby is not sound and healthy; he will be different in some way from ordinary people, even though his form and life may appear similar to other people, because his or her parents' minds do not exist in him. This is against nature's flow and it cannot be good.

Even when the egg or the sperm is artificially inseminated into a mother's womb, it is against the ways of heaven if the structure or the system of the egg or the sperm is not right. It is better to adopt than trying to forcibly have a baby through these means.

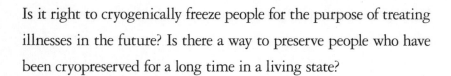

Is it right to cryogenically freeze people for the purpose of treating illnesses in the future? Is there a way to preserve people who have been cryopreserved for a long time in a living state?

It is nature's flow for people to grow old and die, but people continuously strive to live longer. All animals, plants, and things with form in the Universe have a limited lifespan.

It is the way of heaven that breath is essential for everything with a shape - limited but necessary. In other words, it is Truth that all things with form breathe a limited number of breaths and then pass away. However people seek to live forever with the human body and believe there is a way to avoid death because they do not know Truth. Hence, the belief exists that in the future when technology becomes more developed, cryopreserved people will be cured of their illnesses or brought back to life. This is wrong; when people stop breathing, they die.

People believe that if we had perfect cells, we would live forever. However, there is a connection between heaven and man; this connection is the cord of life. Although it cannot be seen with human eyes, when one is able to see with his inner eyes, this cord is distinct, transparent, and clear. It is about the thickness of a finger, but when a person dies this cord breaks.

After a person stops breathing for a certain length of time, he is dead. Therefore, when a person has stopped breathing and is frozen, he dies a natural death. So cryopreservation is impossible. In order to bring him back to life, there must be a saint who can reconnect the cord of life, but only a complete person can do this. Therefore, it is impossible for an ordinary person to make cryopreservation work.

Is the brain responsible for treating illnesses as well as for the body? If the brain is the human mind, what is the whole body of the person?

People originally came from the place of absolute nothingness which exists prior to the existence of people. Of yin and yang in the Universe, man's form exists as yang. But actually yin itself is the original body of the Universe so when people die, they return to yin. Yang simply put into form that which has always originally been in the scope or sphere of yin - all things are simply as they are. This means that something in existence has not pushed out yin when it came into form; even when it is in existence, it is also still yin. Therefore, the human body is a *little Universe* that resembles the Earth. The existence of human form is an expression of yang that came from one's original self which is the Universe. Therefore when it disappears, only the Universe remains just as it is.

The problem is that when man has his own individual mind, he does not disappear completely after death. This human mind resides in the middle brain. In the microcosm of the body, the brain has the role of God and governs over the whole person. It is the mind or the brain that cures illnesses, both curable and incurable. A person's whole body is the mind of the Universe, but the human mind is the brain.

Where is the boundary between life and death, and what criteria decide when a person is dead?

D eath means that a person's life has come to an end. The meaning of the word *life* can be understood from the Korean word, *moksum,* which means *breath in one's throat.* People think that someone is dead only when he has stopped breathing. The problem is that sometimes a person may be breathing, but he is living a life that is the same as being dead. There are some cases where people have recovered from these conditions through being shocked, so it is difficult to set a clear boundary between life and death. Therefore, as of now the only possible way to decide whether a person is dead is to rely on the current medical definition of death.

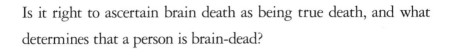

Is it right to ascertain brain death as being true death, and what determines that a person is brain-dead?

B rain death is, when a person's brain is dead. It is impossible to resuscitate a brain-dead person. The brain gives orders to all parts of a person's body and allows him to move, so a person who is brain dead is truly dead. Brain cells that have been damaged due to brain death cannot recover even with medical help.

It is possible for a brain-dead person to breathe when the damaged parts of his brain are unrelated to the parts that allow him to breathe. However, he is still dead. A person's death must be judged carefully and accurately. In any case, when the area of the brain that allows conscious thought and judgment is so severely damaged that it cannot recover, he is brain dead.

Is it right to euthanize a person who is on the brink of death and suffering from great pain? How can his pain be alleviated to ready him for death?

A person's lifespan is tied to heaven, and he himself is heaven. It is natural for him to die. Some people wish to be euthanized because they are suffering from intense pain, but it is not nature's flow to euthanize someone.

There are two types of death: the first kind is one where the person accepts death through nature's flow and the second, an unwanted death full of suffering. However, it is better to leave a person just as he is. There is no way to die without suffering. Accepting death as nature's flow is the closest to dying without suffering.

When a person has committed a crime, what is the right way to punish him in a way that is appropriate to the seriousness of the crime?

The punishment that is given to a person when he commits a crime differs from country to country. In some cases, something that is a crime in one country is not a crime in another. Punishments are man made, and as such they are very inconsistent. It is better to sentence criminals to do hard physical work than putting them in prison. This is because an imprisoned person, who never does anything, can never learn about life.

When people commit crimes to benefit their life, they should be made to repent through living life. Even when a person has committed a brutal crime, he should have the opportunity to repent what he has done through hard labor.

A person can make mistakes and commit crimes in the process of living, but it is nature's flow that he should be helped to not commit the crime again. Punishing him will only make the crime heavier. The ideal way would be to establish an organization to assign hard labor proportionate to the weight of the crime. A person's mind can become cleansed through hard labor and he would not repeat his crimes for fear of the amount of labor he would receive. The quantity of hard labor given to criminals should be decided fairly by age and health, and when the period of hard labor is over, they should be returned to society. There should be regulated working and sleeping hours and those who work hard should be given a chance to end their sentence early.

Why are prophecies about human life wrong?

There are two types of prophecies: prophecies about nature's flow of the Universe and prophecies about human life. Prophecies about the Universe are Truth so they are correct but because human life is not of the true world, prophecies about human life are not Truth. This is because human life itself is false and not true. What is true resides in non-existence where absolutely everything has ceased, so in terms of Truth, it is illogical that someone can know what will happen in a person's life in advance.

Although a shaman's prophecy is sometimes right, it is inconsequential because human life itself is false from the viewpoint of Truth. Therefore, one should not be too attached to prophecies which are not true.

How can we settle the conflict between Israel and the Arabian states?

I srael never fell despite many wars with the Arabic states because Israel is the country chosen by Heaven before the coming of Truth. Israel never lost in war because Heaven had already decided which country will win. Even if Israel had fought with a bigger country, Israel would have not lost. The war in the Middle East is due to conflicting ideologies and religions. Wars are frequent because people are ignorant of Truth and did not know that religions are ultimately one.

Up until now many people have died because of religion. It is because people separate *you* and *me*. The current religious system cannot resolve the conflict in the Middle East. Here are the ways to resolve the conflict.

The first is to teach people that their religions ultimately pursue the same goal, although they seem to be different depending on their locations. Jesus and the saints taught the same Truth to people, but people could not unite because people in different places understood Truth differently and served God differently.

The second is to discard one's long established, customary way of thinking in order to unite ideologies and systems. Since it is difficult to be free from a fixed concept, ideologies and systems should unite to be in peace.

The third way to peace is to rid the gap between the rich and the poor. Once the world starts becoming peaceful, people will unite ideologies and systems, and make peace arrive earlier.

What will happen to the world's economy and politics in the future?

There are many different countries in the world at present, but in the future they will all become one - the whole world will become one, which is completion. There will be no *other* nations, no racial discrimination, and no matter where one goes all people will be like brothers. As a result, world politics will also become complete.

In the past, power was gained through military force, but now the power struggle has become an economic battle. In the near future, the world economy will come to a standstill which will be impossible to revive without becoming complete.

The world economy in the present state will come to an end after a series of tumultuous events, and only nations that follow nature's flow will survive. Products will be made and profit will be gained according to nature's flow; nations that gain profit through dumping or cheap labor will steadily decline and in the end only nations that become Truth will remain.

How can the wrongs of the world be righted?

Until now the world was at an age when people made other people's lives difficult. However, the great *dō* or path will arrive and this age will naturally disappear through nature's flow. Nature's flow has no obstacles, and it will dissolve the conflicts like the flow of water.

People are originally one, without *you* or *me*, but became separated through things such as ethnicity, philosophy, and ideology, and began to envy and fight with each other. Becoming one is to become complete, and everyone will now learn how to become one.

People must be taught the great *dō* which is Truth. The people of the world must learn to move nations and interact with people through this complete Truth and this path is the only way for people in the world to live.

Part 5

Life · Afterlife

Each creation has its own lifespan. Lifespans are decided by the forms they are given when creations are made from the original body - the origin of the Universe. Nothing in the world with form is everlasting. This is Truth.

What is the process and origin of creation?

Everything is created with a form that is appropriate for its surroundings. Creation happens through earth, water, fire, and wind - these things are the source of creation and all things return to them eventually.

All things go through this creation process, but nothing is added to the Universe or subtracted from it; the Universe is as it is. People believe that creation has happened when something comes into being but this is not creation; it is as it is and has always been. For example, when coal is made into nylon its form and traits may change, but its source is still the same.

All things did not come into being from nothing. Rather, what has appeared with form is false and the metaphysical substance is what is real. All things came into existence from the original existence: there was no creation that happened. In other words, all things come from the metaphysical substance and return to it. All celestial bodies form by the exhalation of God, the universe, and they disappear by the inhalation of God.

Why do all things in the world appear from yin and yang?

E verything in the world is comprised of yin and yang. This
is because one's existence is originally yin and yang. Yin
refers to that which cannot originally be seen, and yang refers to
that which we can see with our eyes. We were originally yin but
yang appeared from yin, and yang in turn conceived all things in
the world. Some things in the world are made of yang, and some
are made of yin. Yin and yang are the fundamental elements of
creation and if they did not exist, living creatures would not be
able to procreate. This is nature's flow.

Yin and yang are the highest existences in the world, but the
creations that are made through yin and yang disappear of and
by themselves after a certain period of time. People call this
a lifespan. Many people have come and gone from the world
since mankind appeared on Earth but the weight and volume
of the Earth remain constant. It is best for yin and yang to be
in balance, and yin and yang co-exist for each other. One is not
higher than the other; they are equal.

Although all beings are the same, the origin consists of yin and yang and therefore the basic elements of creation also consist of yin and yang. The Earth is yang, but all things are created through heaven (the sky) which is yin. This is the law and principle of heaven. The appearance of yin and yang with form is nature's flow.

Why did heaven create people?

Humans are not made by God or by humans, nor do they appear on their own. Human is God, human is earth, and human is everything. The real identity of the Universe is simply that which exists as it is. If we had to speak of a reason people were created, it would be that they were made to govern over all creations. Specifically, people were made to rule over creations and live according to nature's flow. However, the human world is a problem because people do not do so.

In other words, man and creations are one and the same but man was made to govern over creations. This means that he should use all things in creation so that all people can live fair and equal lives, and not so that he can use them for his own greed. All things are heaven itself, and heaven or the sky is absolutely fair. People should also share fairly and equally, and govern over all creations according to nature's flow. This is the reason heaven created people.

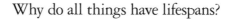

Why do all things have lifespans?

E ach creation has its own lifespan. Lifespans are decided by the forms they are given when creations are made from the original body - the origin of the Universe. In other words, having a material form is in itself a lifespan. Nothing in the world with form is everlasting, only the length of each form's lifespan differs. This is Truth.

What is destiny, and is it possible to know one's destiny in advance?

P eople have many things to do, and they do many things. Many people wonder about their fate or destiny; they want to know what their destiny is but they are unable to gain any clear answers. This is because people are controlled by their minds, but humans are fickle and change frequently. A person's thoughts in the morning changes by nightfall, only to change again by the next morning.

The reason behind man's curiosity about his fate comes from his ignorance of where he comes from and where he will return to after he dies. It is from the original nothingness that man came; this place of nothingness is the place of Truth. When he knows Truth - the place of emptiness and the reason it created all things - his questions will disappear. Not knowing Truth is like being in the darkness so it is natural that man finds life a mystery. Destiny is not something that originally exists; one simply comes into existence by moving into a state of having form. The problem is that man desires to know why this is so.

Man is an existence that drifts like a cloud within the flow of changing time. Not knowing that he is a cloud-like existence, he desires to become the master of the cloud. Consequently, he himself creates his destiny and then suffers because he finds his destiny difficult to bear. Man is like the moon that drifts with the clouds but he tries to stop both the moon and the clouds from drifting; this is what creates his destiny.

Many people hope that their destiny will be a great one, but not many people actually have a great destiny. Therefore, most people live in suffering. Their destiny is tied to heaven, and although they try to escape it, it cannot be changed. One should accept his destiny because trying to forcedly change it often brings about an even worse fate. In any case, destiny is something that both exists and does not exist: it does not exist because it is something that is already decided, yet at the same time it exists because it can be changed by one's actions.

The only way to become completely free of one's fate or change a bad fate into a good one is to become enlightened and know Truth. There are no restrictions when one becomes Truth; no hindrances of any kind. This is the original meaning of what people call destiny.

What is the I Ching?

The I Ching is a divinatory text of the Zhou dynasty in China. The laws of celestial bodies in the universe, mathematics, and people's fortunes are academically divined based on its writings. The I Ching covers everything from astronomy and philosophy to mathematics, and it contains the studies of the best scholars of the time.

Some of its contents are correct, but it is not perfection. Being a highly academic text, not only were the expressions in the book difficult to understand back in the days when it was written, it is still extremely difficult to interpret today. There are parts of the book that only the writer himself can understand. While it is similar to Truth, it is not Truth itself.

What is *The Secrets of Master Tojeong?*

It is a book written by Yi Jiham which explains people's destiny based on the knowledge in the I Ching. It attempts to explain people's fortune by their birth dates and times, based on the twelve animals of Heaven. This is statistically close to real, but it is not perfect. If something is not perfection, it is not correct; if it is not correct it is unnecessary.

An individual's destiny changes from time to time because human mind changes frequently. In order to ascertain a person's scope, we need to know the size of the person's mind. But in reality, we cannot understand the range, so no one knows people's destiny; only perfection knows.

What is astrology?

During ancient times in the West, people used the constellations to predict the fates of people and nations. The movement of the stars helped people to predict the future at a time when people lived in harmony with nature. Although there is a certain logic behind this practice, it is not always accurate. Truth - something that is right - lasts through the ages but that which is false disappears. The reason astrology has become irrelevant is because it is not always right. The science of astrology came from the misunderstanding that there was a shepherd who could foresee the future by looking at the stars. In reality, he was enlightened of the laws of the universe and engaged in dialogue with heaven.

Man's fate and future does not rest in the stars, but they have an influence on fate; similar to the way the Earth cannot exist alone but depends on the strength and existence of other stars.

What is the difference between the phrases, "He has died" and "He has returned"?

The phrase "He has died" refers to a person who no longer breathes - someone whose life has come to an end. The expression "He has returned" is a Korean euphemism for death. It means that man came from the emptiness of non-existence - where originally there is absolutely nothing - and that he has returned to this emptiness. This expression was coined by those who knew Truth.

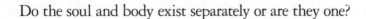

Do the soul and body exist separately or are they one?

People make distinctions between the soul and the physical body but they are one; they do not exist separately. Nothing remains when a person whose soul and body are one dies. Such a person has achieved the state or level of the original self that is the Universe. Not knowing this, man himself makes a soul which remains when he dies. He suffers because he cannot see the original body of the Universe which is covered up by this soul.

A person just as he is, is the appearance of his original self. He exists as he is even when his form disappears. However man believes that everything disappears when he dies. Having a proper understanding of this through enlightenment is the study of *dō* (the Way) and it is Truth. Man exists as he is - he neither lives nor dies.

What happens after death, and is there a difference between what happens to a child and an adult?

When a child dies, his soul acts like the child that he was. A young soul does not know where to go, and often remains by his house or mother. Even an adult who dies before the end of his lifespan has a tendency to stay near his house because of his attachments.

A person who dies at the end of his lifespan is able to find his way not long after his death because he does not have regrets. However, a person whose life is cut short because of an accident or illness wanders the area of his death or the netherworld because of the regrets about his life.

The majority of people behave in the same way after death as when they were alive. They are unable to return to their true self by nature's flow because they do not know what death is. This is the reason one must be enlightened while he is living so that he can live in the Universe during his life and after his death. This is the best way - to return to Truth that is one's true self.

We dedicate ourselves to making money, but we are thoroughly negligent about finding our eternal selves. This is the reason we suffer after death - because we do not know Truth. Truth never changes or disappears, but if we do not find it while we are living there is no guarantee that we will find it after death. Even if it is possible, it would be extremely difficult. We must pay more attention and try harder to find our true selves while we are living.

What is the difference between heaven and hell? How does a ghost of the dead live in heaven or in hell?

Heaven is a house in the sky, while hell is a house on earth. A person who is not bound to commandment and whose mind is free from burdens goes to heaven. A person who does not obey commandment goes to hell, on his own. People in heaven live in comfort because burdens do not exist. A life in hell is suffering because it is laden with burdens. Burdens exist in the mind - people take that mind when they die. Namely, they send themselves to hell by making karma and sins. Religions have always bound people in the notions of sins and karma, but they do not exist. The study of Truth is the realization that there are no sins and karma. No one would have gone to hell if religions had taught people that sins and karma do not exist - this is the reason hell exists, and people go to hell after death. Hell now no longer exists. Life is suffering enough - it is against the ways of heaven to make another separate hell and make man suffer further. It is not nature's flow. Man's immature actions during his life cannot become sins and karma.

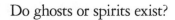

Do ghosts or spirits exist?

G hosts or spirits are a type of thought-mass which is formed from imagined thoughts. Ghosts have actually existing form although they are thought-masses, and it is possible to see them either when one is feeling very depressed or when he has absolutely no self.

There are peaceful ghosts but there are also those that are angry and bitter. These angry and bitter ghosts become spirits. Spirits are souls that had unresolved bitterness and anger when they were alive. There are ghosts and spirits everywhere but people live unaware of them because they are invisible to human eyes.

Are ghost marriages effective?

The souls of dead single people still desire to get married because they mistakenly believe they are still alive. Their preferences for a partner are similar to the preferences of living people. Family members arrange these ghost marriages because they fear that the souls of the deceased have regrets about their single status, but the souls themselves rarely go through with these arranged marriages. Although a rare few do get married, the majority do not agree with the choice of partner their families have arranged for them because of their remaining human habits and preferences. The souls themselves must want the marriage to happen. Although one or two out of a hundred of these marriages actually happen, ghost marriages are so ineffective that they are the same as not arranging them at all.

What is the afterworld like?

People believe that they will exist in the afterworld in a similar way to the way they are while they are alive. However, this is not the case. That one exists means the same as that one does not exist; but this means that he does exist. He exists if he takes his habits and tendencies with him after death but if he discards all of them, he does not exist.

To take one's habits and tendencies with him into death means he takes all the sufferings he had when he was living. It is Truth and nature's flow to cease to exist after death; living with self only furthers his suffering. When one has no self, he is not bound or tied to any place because he is the Universe. This is the afterworld.

Can man reincarnate as an animal, object, or tree through *samsara* - the cycle of birth and death?

Man believes that he is different from animals and inanimate objects because he has intelligence and life, but in fact he is the animals and inanimate objects. All creations are one, but there are millions of different forms in creation. They are categorized as animal, plant, and inanimate object, and they have different traits and behaviors as well as having a name. Man seeks to know everything but human intelligence and wisdom has limitations.

There are no rules to a person's reincarnation because all things are one. In other words, he could be reborn as anything. A person is a human being only because he was born as a human being but he came from non-existence, returns to non-existence, and he can be reborn as any of the other creations through his ties and karma, whether it be a stone or something else.

There are largely four places people go after death. First, they could go to the original body. Second, they could follow the karma that they have amassed (whether it be heaven or hell). Third, he could remain drifting in the netherworld. Fourth, he could remain in the netherworld for a while and then be reborn in heaven.

These are the places that man goes to after death. When man dies, his mind (his soul) remains. When this mind enters another entity, it again has form. This process is called reincarnation.

Are life forms such as plant seeds, fruit, and fish eggs created through *samsara*, the cycle of death and rebirth?

Among the countless individual life forms such as flower seeds, fruit, and fisheggs, there are many which were not created through samsara. The reason for this is plant seeds exist because the plant exists, and fish eggs and fruit exist because the fish and tree exist. Therefore, the plant seeds, fish eggs, and fruit are not an individual entity, but a part of a whole.

They are the whole organism - they were not created through samsara. When they are separated from the whole and become individual entities themselves, they gain individual selves which then go through samsara. When they are with the original organism, they are a part of it.

Simply put, a seed and a fruit is the same as the tree, and a fish egg is the same as the fish. When they are separated as individuals later, they come to have their own minds of and by themselves. These individual minds make them go through samsara.

When an animal dies, where does its soul go? Is a slaughterhouse full of dead animals' souls?

When animals die, their souls do not know where to go. They stay near the place they used to live and after a period of time, they realize by themselves that they are not needed and they leave. Animals killed at a slaughterhouse have regrets that they died without knowing where they must go after death, and the majority stay in the slaughterhouse. All life forms gives off an evil energy when they die. In order for that evil energy to dissipate, they need to be given rites of passage to heaven. It is a shame this is not done for them.

These souls remain for a period of time and then leave. They wander where they like for awhile and after time passes, and when it is time for them to be reincarnated, these souls become very small masses, the shape of a sperm, which wander around in the air. This is the stage before they are reincarnated.

What is an out-of-body experience?

Man has a mind that looks exactly like his body. It exists but it cannot be seen with human eyes - it is clear, transparent, and invisible. However, a person with no minds is able to see it because he has no minds. It is a mind form, so it behaves in the same way as a mind form of the real substance. Therefore, the rules of time and space do not apply to it.

It can go to any corner of the Universe within moments, and move in a flash. It can become separated from the human body and move freely to deliver messages. This is an out-of-body experience. Even when one is alive, if he is able to move this mind-form it can freely come and go from heaven and know heaven's messages. The mind has no past, present, or future, so he can know the past. Time and space does not exist in the mind. When one dies, this mind-form becomes what people call a soul. However, if one eliminates this mind and it disappears, he becomes a great sage - a person of freedom without hindrances. People with clear minds can have out-of-body experiences at will.

What is the world of souls like, and what differences does it have from the world of gods?

The world of souls is a place where souls that died with their remaining individual minds gather and live after death. There are five different levels of souls.

First, there are souls that have not been enlightened at all. Second, there are souls that have been enlightened a little. Third, there are souls that have been half-enlightened. Fourth, there are souls that have been enlightened a lot and lastly, there are fully enlightened souls.

Enlightenment is knowing Truth, but the enlightenment of souls is a level of enlightenment where he has not achieved spiritual death. This level of enlightenment is simply knowing the place of the mind. They still have selves, and therefore they have not been liberated. They live lives mistakenly thinking that all things exist. The human heaven is a sort of transitional institution for edification for souls that have yet to be enlightened, and it takes a long time for them to achieve full spiritual death. These souls must become enlightened by themselves so it takes a long period of time without any guarantee of when it will happen.

Very few souls reach even the human heaven while most wander hell or purgatory, unable to let go of the attachments to the lives they lived with suffering in the human world. They are unable to let go because they mistake human life as being real.

Gods are those who have achieved full enlightenment. Full enlightenment is the state when one is completely without self. He is not restricted to any place because this state is the Universe. He is completely liberated. A person who has no self is completely free. Therefore, gods can have forms and save people. Though they live together with people, they live without individual minds. This state of mind is the mind of the Universe.

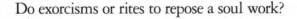

Do exorcisms or rites to repose a soul work?

When a person dies, his soul follows his ties and karma. Rites to repose a soul are carried out to help the deceased forget his ties and karma, because when a person dies with attachments to his ties and karma he is unable to leave. Although this practice makes sense, most of the time it does not work.

These rites and exorcisms should be carried out by a person who has achieved full enlightenment. This was not possible in the time before the coming of Truth; in the time after the coming of Truth all souls will cease to have karma and ties and they will be able to go to heaven as gods. When a person becomes enlightened, he will live in heaven eternally.

Can a soul go to heaven after death if he is given the Buddhist service of forty-nine days of prayers, or if he is given the prayers of passage to heaven?

People pray for forty-nine days in a temple after a person dies because it is thought that this will help the soul of the deceased to go to heaven. However this practice does not work because the soul does not know where heaven is. It is the same for prayers of passage to heaven because the person performing the prayers does not know where to send him. However, these practices serve as a consolation to the deceased's loved ones so it is fine to do them. Now, anyone can go to the land of God and Buddha after he dies. Even when one is still alive, he can go to heaven if he is completely without self.

What is possession?

Possession is when a soul other than one's own enters his body. When a person becomes possessed he becomes another person's mind that is not his own. If you observe people closely, you can see many people who do not act like themselves and do things they do not intend to do. This is because another soul has entered him - he has been possessed.

A dead person's soul tries to fulfill his unfulfilled desires from his life by entering his descendants or other people. Possessed people suffer greatly-often becoming mentally ill and sometimes becoming insane. Illnesses that even hospitals do not know the cause of are usually caused by possession. The best way to cure such illnesses is to send the immature attached soul to heaven. Then the patient will be cured.

What is the reason some people become spiritual mediums or fortune tellers?

A person becomes a spiritual medium when he is invaded by another soul or spirit. This does not pose a problem for someone who has become one with his real self, but when a soul enters the body of a person who has not become one with his real self, he suffers greatly. Some spirits enter a spiritual medium's body to resolve anger or to carry out their desires. The person becomes a medium and he is controlled by that spirit. This is what a spiritual medium is.

When a person's mind is weakened and loses its foundation another soul can come in. This is called possession. Everyone is influenced by their ancestors because man is born with a mind that resembles his ancestors. When an unenlightened spirit desires to carry out its unfulfilled will it enters someone until they are no longer useful, at which point it moves on and enters its children and descendants. Hereditary spiritual mediums are such cases.

A prediction or prophecy made by a spiritual medium is not done by the medium himself but by the spirit that possesses him. The mind has no past, present, or future so the human mind can appear like an image. The spirit possessing a spiritual medium uses these images to make predictions. Some prophecies turn out to be correct, but many are not.

What is basic human instinct?

B asic human instinct is the original mind that is innate in people. This original mind is omnipotent and omniscient, so this mind governs how he lives in the world.

This mind is omnipotent and omniscient because it exists of and by itself. A person is complete and perfect in himself - because a human itself is perfection. Therefore, although no one teaches them, as humans they just know how to eat, live, and have children. Basic human instinct is not something that is learned; it is the original ability to do things of and by one's self.

What is the difference between a pessimistic and optimistic outlook on life?

A person has an optimistic outlook on life when he has hope, and when he does not his viewpoint is pessimistic.

Hope is wishing for something, and when its achievement looks possible one is optimistic but when it does not seem possible, he is pessimistic. This happens in the mind. Therefore optimistic people are more likely to succeed. This is because the conviction that something can happen drives him to succeed. In any case, optimism and pessimism is a by-product of the human mind.

People often talk about luck and fortune. Is luck simply a fortunate coincidence or do people win the lottery because it has been pre-decided?

When something good unexpectedly happens to someone, he believes it is luck. The meaning of luck is a happy fortune and luck gives joy that is free of worries. This joy does not indiscriminately come to someone; it comes to him through his karmic ties.

Karmic ties are when something follows a connection or a relationship for a reason. For example, a person can win the lottery because he bought a lottery ticket. The winning follows this action. Such luck is pre-decided. This is because coincidence is not really coincidence, it is an event of inevitability; an event of inevitability is a matter of course. A matter of course is something that is already decided.

What should man learn from nature?

M an is nature and nature is man; all creations are man and man is all of creation. People are blind; they can only see what they see, and therefore have discernment between this and that. However, if there were a lesson that man could learn from water, it would be that water exists in accordance with nature's flow. It is not stubborn or obstinate; it exists simply as it is. Man should learn nature's flow from water. All things in nature are simply as they are, but only man makes a self and constantly builds up and destroys delusions that arise from his shape and form. Therefore he must learn from nature, which is silently subservient.

Everything in the world is one, but people have given names to each different form and try to judge them by their traits or movements. However, they should know that all things are one.

What is energy (*qi* or *chi*)?

E nergy refers to the power of the entire Universe. Although we distinguish between the emptiness, animate and inanimate objects, all things in creation subsist through this energy. Whether it be the earth, the emptiness, man, animal, or other living creatures, they all consist of this energy.

Originally energy flows and moves smoothly in all things, but energy channels can become blocked because of individual minds which all animate and inanimate creatures have. Everything in the world is energy, and the emptiness itself is energy. All things exist because of energy, therefore energy is completeness and perfection.

What came first, the chicken or the egg?

T he chicken came first. From the viewpoint of Truth, it is the principle of the world that all things on Earth begin with their complete or mature forms. This is because animals and all things in nature can procreate only when they are complete. So a chicken must be a complete chicken. Only when a chicken exists could it lay eggs. It is not the case that an egg brought forth a chicken.

The chicken came from a complete place. A complete place refers to a place where there is absolutely nothing, a place where everything has ceased; the entire Universe. Nothing is impossible from this place, and it is from here that all things are created.

Part 6

Religion · Salvation

Originally man did not have sins. Sins and karma came to exist when man began to live only for his own survival, and they cease to exist when his self does not exist. That one's self does not exist means he is no longer controlled by his self and that he has found his real self - the original self. Such a person does not have original sin because he does not dwell in his life though he is alive, and he does not reside in his daily life though he lives each day.

What is religion?

Religion is following someone's teachings. Religion has had a tremendous psychological influence on people. Although it has helped people in some ways, it has also been a source of loss. For example, because people are blind to Truth they began to discriminate against other religions which, among other things, led to religious wars. Religion is about blind faith, but in reality there is no meaning in blind faith. Religion must have Truth - one must seek and practice Truth along with faith.

Something has gone wrong when people become more attached to supposed miracles while Truth takes a backseat. Truth does not reside in miracles or wonders; it resides in nature's flow.

Anything that is not true is completely false. Religions spoke to people about the existence of God, and although this has helped people, Truth does not dwell in words. Neither can it be found in books or scriptures. There have been many saints in the world; they were sent by heaven during different points in history depending on changes in social conditions. But their heroic values and actions often became exaggerated as people embellished the miracles and mysteries attributed to the saints. Moreover, there are many different interpretations of their words and actions because no one had the inner eyes to be able to correctly interpret them. Inner eyes refers to the mind's eyes and if people's minds' eyes have not opened, their interpretations of Truth are bound to differ. In many cases, these interpretations are not Truth and become the cause behind religions splitting off into new denominations and sects.

Religions in the time before the coming of Truth were not perfect; people in different religions fought because they did not know that Truth is one and the same. Now, the way to great enlightenment has opened. All people are one, and therefore everyone around us, the entire world, will become one. Religions will also unite in the future and the world will finally become a peaceful place. All people will live equal lives and all will receive salvation.

Why do many religions prosper in Korea?

Hankook, which is the Korean word for Korea, also means
a big country. Korea is a great country for many religions
from around the world to prosper in because conditions in
Korea have always been unstable due to frequent invasions by
other countries. Therefore, people favored religions because they
teach that people can at least go to a good place after death, and
they will live there forever; hence many people came to believe
those religions. Furthermore, Koreans favored foreign religions
because they came from countries stronger and wealthier than
Korea. The result, as we see now, is that many religions have
prospered in Korea.

Religions are divided into many denominations; and this
imperfect state gives rise to an imperfect situation. The result
is that instead of Truth the thoughts of individuals became the
power that made the religion spread even more.

Since people do not know Truth, they do not know what is
right and what is wrong. Because people are ignorant of Truth,

pseudo-religions, or cults, which satisfy people's thoughts, have become common. In fact, these false religions have a louder voice in today's society. Truth is not in outspoken words. Truth does not reside in appearance. Truth is not about a certain person.

What is a false religion?

A false religion is similar to the real thing but it is not the genuine article.

False religions have become commonplace because people do not know Truth and consequently they are easily fooled. Truth is something that is never-changing and there is only one Truth, which is the mind. This mind was called God, Buddha, and Allah in different religions. Although these names sound different, they all refer to the same existence. False religions display the following misguided behaviors:

False religions intimidate people in the name of God.

False religions worship false idols.

False religions lead people to believe in ideologies that are wrong.

False religions ask for money.

False religions put off educating people about Truth.

False religions set goals that are never achieved.

False religions make people believe in one certain God.

False religions do not know Truth so they emphasize blind faith.

False religions claim that their religion is the best.

False religions claim that one's life or fate can suddenly change.

False religions confuse people with trivial miracles or wonders.

False religions decorate their surroundings lavishly.

False religions cannot distinguish between what is true and what is false.

False religions act falsely and have no results.

Even if a false religion becomes free of all of the above behaviors, it is still a false religion if it does not have the seal that is the origin of the Universe. If it does not have the Truth of the Universe, it is a false religion.

Negative consequences from improper religions abusing people have become serious. For example, there are religions that build lavish and opulent buildings for themselves but neglect charity work for the poor. Why is this?

A n *improper* religion is a religion where Truth does not exist although it may seem as though it does. Religious books were written by people who were not enlightened and many statements about Truth were expressed wrongly, all of which severely hindered people's understanding of Truth. Truth is not in a book. Nor is it in scriptures. The world of God and Buddha is that which just exists - this is also one's real self. However people are unable to find Truth because they search for it outside of themselves. One himself is God and Buddha. Man himself is God, but he does not know this because he is not enlightened.

The reason people cannot see God even when their eyes are open is one can see God only when he has died and he no longer exists; when his mind and body, and even his soul have disappeared. The reason people have religion is in order to see

God and go to the land of God. However, faith alone cannot ever bring them to the land of God.

Religions have manipulated people's fears about the end of the world for their own ends. While they decorate their surroundings in a grand way, they do not have any real substance. The Savior they wish for will never appear, even when the end of the world comes; and if he did appear he would not stay. Luxurious buildings and lavish surroundings are wasteful. They have no meaning because Truth does not exist in these things. Since Truth does not exist in these religions, they do not have the inclination to help people. Even when they do, their actions are done with human minds so it does not end up helping people at all. Real Truth does not sparkle or shine, but it is everlasting.

In the Middle Ages, people believed that the soul was under the jurisdiction of God, while the body was under the jurisdiction of the material world. Asceticism emerged because people thought physical pleasure was sinful and a depravity. Due to this, many clergymen did not get married. Were they right?

I t is completeness for people to live together. It is not nature's flow for a person to live unmarried in order for him, alone, to be enlightened. From the viewpoint of Truth, the unity of man and woman is completeness. Suppressing one's desires and leaving the roots of those desires in his mind is worse than actually getting married. The difference between getting married and living alone is that when one practices asceticism, the mind of suppression exists. When one does not suppress his desires, he does not have this mind. Therefore, he is more easily able to get to heaven.

When God made man, he made him perfect as a human being. A person cannot artificially be made to become God; his mind must be eliminated completely. Furthermore, it is not just man's soul but also his body belongs to God, because man is God and God is man.

The *soul* is an individual's mind mass - it is a person's mind. A person who takes his mind with him into death cannot enter the land of God. Such a person can only go to the heaven in the land of souls, which is a place where souls with a *self* who could not enter the true heaven of God gather and live. When one's soul itself disappears, he can go to the land of gods - the complete land of God.

How was Christianity able to prevail over ancient philosophy, elevate itself to a superior spiritual position and spread all over the world? Why can it not unite all other religions in the world?

Christianity was able to prevail over ancient philosophy, elevate itself to a superior spiritual position and spread itself around the world because it had the salvation ideology. It was also helped by the spread of Western culture and civilization around the world. However, European Christianity which flourished in the Middle Ages has now reached its limits because it is not perfection.

Countries which took in Christianity did so because of its superior culture but its progress will tail off after a certain period of time. The Christian ideology had many blockages or hitches; it was about sacrifice and love but people found it difficult to carry it out in practice. When an ideology is not perfection, it is bound to have hitches and blockages; all religions are imperfect religions.

The cross became a symbol for Christianity after Jesus Christ died by crucifixion. What is the meaning behind this symbol?

The cross represents endlessness, both vertically and horizontally. The Buddhist swastika also represents endlessness.

Did the flesh and blood of Christ actually change into the Host and sacred blood (sacramental bread and wine)? And what happens when one eats and drinks them?

The Host and sacred blood is said to be Jesus Christ because he was a person who had achieved the state of non-existence, a state without self. In other words, as a person of Truth, anything can become the Host and sacred blood, not just bread and wine. As he is a person of Truth, he taught that everything exists within him and that it is the same as eternal life.

The Host and sacred blood is represented by bread and wine; when it is taken with the devout faith that it is Christ's flesh and blood, it can bring about a miracle. A miracle is something that happens when one does not have any individual minds; when one has become one with Jesus Christ. Simply put, a person can become one with Jesus Christ and God when he is completely without self. It is because people do not know this that they think of themselves and Christ and God as being separate.

When one has strong faith and acts accordingly, miracles can happen, though they differ according to the form of the person's ego or self. Anyone can eat and drink the bread and wine but the result varies from person to person.

What is Adam and Eve's original sin spoken of in the Bible?

The life one lives comes from being born as a human being and it is through his life that man comes to have sin, of and by himself. Originally, man is an existence that has absolutely nothing, but since he makes sins and karma of and by himself and he has to live bearing their burden, this can be called original sin. Man did not originally have sins. Sins and karma came to exist when man began to live for his own survival, and they cease to exist when his self does not exist. That one's self does not exist means he is no longer controlled by his self and that he has found his real self - the original self. Such a person does not have original sin because he does not dwell in his life though he is alive, and he does not reside in his daily life though he lives each day.

Therefore, it is wrong to say that man has original sin. Life itself is sin, but one does not have sin. A person's origin is neither good nor evil; it is non-existence. It is said that acting for one's survival or his existence is sin but even this does not exist. Man has sins because people are not enlightened. Man does not have sin.

A person is simply a person, and all creations are simply what they are-no more and no less, and they do not have any sins or karma. One can be liberated from these conceptions completely when one knows Truth.

What does the Bible tell us?

The Old Testament is a type of legend. Even if its contents are correct, it is difficult for people to interpret correctly, which they cannot do. Truth must be taken in exactly and just as it is; if it is misinterpreted one runs the risk of becoming an eternally lost child of Truth.

It is best to see both the Old and New Testaments as prophecies. The final message in these prophecies is that a Savior will come. This Savior is a complete being who is omnipotent and omniscient, and he is a person who can eliminate all creations in the world and enable them to go to the land of God. In the time before the coming of Truth, religions did not have true salvation that allows people to go to the land of God. They simply spoke of the fact that the land of God is near, and waited for completion to come. To be called complete, it must be complete for eternity.

People often become scared because they believe devils or demons exist. Do they actually exist?

D evils or demons do not exist. A demon is a person who teaches people something that is not Truth or an immature soul who bewitches people. A person who commits the worst sin is one who lures people and guides them down the wrong path for his own benefit. A person who teaches something that is not Truth makes his students' souls unclean, and such a person's soul is no different from a demon.

People watch horror movies with vampires, but these things do not exist. If they did exist, they are simply people who have become insane - they do not really exist.

Spirits sometimes appear in front of people whose states of mind have become extremely low, and they are called devils. However, they are made by human minds and do not actually exist.

What meaning does Catholic confession have?

Confession is a means of shedding the burden in one's mind, and as such, it has a purpose. However, the confession must be a true one, and one must not have any minds about his confession. Confession has a similar effect as repentance but it does not necessarily have to be done in this manner. When one deeply reflects back on himself and discards his minds, it is the same as going to confession.

What is the purpose behind the practice of calling out *mea culpa* during Catholic prayers to aid repentance and penitence?

D ue to corrupted politics, people lost their faith in the world where wrong doing is justified. So they said mea culpa which means my fault, not to blame others but to blame themselves. It is a virtue in the human world; but it is not right because when a person thinks he is guilty and is sinful, the blame on himself becomes his original sin. Humans originally do not have any sin. Yet it is wrong to take on oneself a sin with its responsibilities when he is innocent.

Originally, we do not have any sins and karma. This is because we came from the real substance of the Universe, and when we disappear and return to this existence sins no longer exist. However, our own minds make our sins and karma, as well as controlling and restricting ourselves - this is the reason sins and karma exist. People began saying *mea culpa* in order to point out the deeds of corrupt politicians who justified their actions.

This phrase is a virtue of the human world, but it is wrong to unconditionally blame oneself when he did nothing wrong.

What is the best way to repent and do penitence correctly?

The fastest way for someone to eliminate and be absolved of their sins through repentance and penitence is to discard himself completely. Second, he must eliminate his individual self. Third, he must repent sincerely. Fourth, he must not allow even this sincerity to remain in his mind. Fifth, there must be nothing that he is hiding. Sixth, he must vomit out everything in his mind through nature's flow. Seventh, he must eliminate absolutely everything from his mind. This is the truthful and sincere way to do repentance and penitence.

In Christianity, it is said that Jesus Christ will save a person who is in despair if he prays earnestly through a testimony or confession of faith, or he will give him a revelation or blessing. Why does this happen? Isn't it better to be religious if these kinds of miracles happen to those who believe in Christ?

I t is not through God but through the discovery of their original self that these revelations or blessings happen. The discovery of the original self happens when one is completely without self, and sometimes it appears when he is earnestly testifying or confessing.

The original self is omnipotent and omniscient; it is without past, present, or future so there is nothing that it does not know. It is because we do not know Truth that such experiences are called the revelations of Christ or God. When none of one's self exists, it is possible to see God. That God is one's self. Therefore, revelations happen when a person completely transforms into his original self. Such revelations can happen at times, not through Truth but through his own hopes, love, ambitions, and prayers.

Sometimes people call this a blessing. Religion was necessary in an incomplete society but completion is the discovery of one's original self. Now, it is the time to discover one's original self instead of blindly believing in a religion. If this happens, he can know all Truth, he will not have any blockages, and he will come to know everything he was curious about, just like clouds being cleared from the sky. A religion where one prays for blessings or blindly believes is not Truth. Anyone can become God and Buddha; people do not know this because they are covered by their human minds. All people are the noble existence that is God and Buddha.

Is it true that Jesus Christ will come again in 1996, two thousand years after his birth?

C hristian stories that tell us the Messiah will come two thousand years after the birth of Christ are true. A Savior must be truly a Savior. A Savior must know the land of God, and he must be able to guide all people and all creations to the land of God; only then can he be called a Savior. Therefore, none of the previous saints have been Saviors.

People do not know Truth, so they get upset when they are told that all creations and man are God, but the land of God does not exist somewhere separately. Originally man was the Universe before he became a human being. However, he lives a self-centered life unaware of the Universe, his original self, because of his individual mind. He may believe the land of God exists somewhere else, but such a place exists only in his thoughts.

Man's life itself is false, but the human mind is unable to let go of its attachments to life. Therefore his soul remained even after death and he suffered. Now, it is nature's flow to get rid of one's self completely so that he can enter the complete land of God. Those who are enlightened will do the work of heaven while they are here on Earth in a state of complete selflessness, and such people will live forever in heaven as gods. This is the new heaven that the Savior has made. Furthermore, it is a new earth because the work of a person who works for heaven is fulfilled here also. The will or purpose behind the appearance of the Savior is to make heaven, earth, and man one, so that they may live in the land of God while they are alive, as well as after death.

It is said that there will be a period of hardships and ordeals before the end of the world comes. Is it currently such a time?

T he end of the world is something that is always present. The issue is what the standard for the end of the world is. Originally the end of the world and a period of hardship do not exist. In any case, it is not currently such a time. The end of the world is a time of chaos when the stars align themselves in a particular way. There is nothing that people can do at this time; they must simply stay as they are. Even if people are told when the end of the world will come, many people would not believe it because they have been fooled numerous times and they do not want to think about any type of misfortune.

What is the meaning of *a religion of fruition?*

Fruition means to bear fruit. It means to return to being a fruit, having begun life as a fruit. A fruit must be a fruit; it is false for something that is not a fruit to try and play the role of a fruit. People came from the original foundation, so it is natural to return to it, but people have made their individual selves which continue to exist in the world of souls even after they die, so this is not Truth.

Fruition means completion; completion is without change, it is without hindrances, it is pure and without greed. To go to heaven after one's death is to travel a road of suffering. The land of God and Buddha that is spoken of in religion is where we came from, and thus it is where we must return to. However man is not able to get there, he holds onto his human mind even after death and wanders the world of his own mind.

In the land of God, heaven, earth, and man should be one. If they exist separately, it is not completion. It is completion only when everything is one, and because there was no one who could make this happen, heaven itself came as a Savior to fulfill this. He will unite all gods in heaven, he will make all heavens unite by eliminating the false heaven (paradise), and he will give spiritual death to all people so that they may go to the land of God. When all gods on earth also disappear, they will go to the land of God so that all things become one.

Because the Savior has already achieved the unity of heaven, earth, and man, when people are enlightened they will live in the land of God while they are living as well as after death. Furthermore, everything man does on earth will be fulfilled in heaven, and he will be resurrected as a god in the land of God. This is the new heaven. This is the *religion of fruition* that will bear fruit, and this fruition is the eternal and boundless Truth.

What is heaven's intention behind the salvation of man?

The intention of heaven behind saving people is for all people to become heaven, so that they can become one. Even though people have the mind of heaven within them, they live with a mind that is not heaven's mind. Therefore they are unable to become one with heaven. The mind they live with is the human mind of greed. However, in the world man is of the highest and the greatest. It is the will of heaven that man lives as a true person and that man lives forever as a human being.

Heaven created man to be complete, without anything lacking. The reason man is not able to be one with heaven is his own greed. Man bears suffering and burden of and by himself and is unable to shed them. Thus, heaven has come to help man become free of his suffering. Heaven pities man, who bears sins and cannot walk the path of salvation. Man has no wisdom; he cannot distinguish between Truth and falseness and he is attached to his futile self image. When he breaks it he can enter the way of Truth. It is hard to distinguish between Truth and falseness, but Truth is absolutely absent of one's self.

Part 7

Poems of Enlightenmen

Existence and non-existence
are simply just one.

Prologue

When heaven and earth are reborn,
when heaven and earth are alive,
it is the new heaven and new earth.

The new heaven and new earth we have only heard about exist;
they exist in the place where the human mind is transformed.

When a person completely becomes God Himself who is
oneness, his mind is oneness; it is the new heaven and new earth.

God is oneness; for Him all things are one.
This is the reason Truth is alive.

Truth is oneness.
When man becomes Truth,
everything lives.
When a person has the land of Truth and God within him,

he lives.

When a person becomes the origin that is Truth,
it is the origin that lives, as Truth itself.
Oneness is to live as completeness.
Oneness is eternal and indestructible
because it is Truth.

Man can live because he is Truth.
Man can live because he is oneness.
All things just live.

What is born is
the existence prior to the human mind -
God, or Buddha.

All things exist in this place,
and they exist, just as they are;
they live as oneness,
as forms of Truth.
Existence and non-existence
are simply just one.

To be one means
everything is oneness itself.

If I die and then am reborn,
all things are reborn as one and Truth
in the whole, that has become my self.
It is then that all things live.

In the place where I have died, everything exists.
All things live because they are one.

A person is Truth only when he has become oneness.
He is Truth when he has gone to Buddha who is oneness.

Such a person is oneness.
He is Truth itself.
When a person has become oneness,
he himself knows that he has;
and it is when his mind returns to oneness
that he knows the true meaning of oneness,
and he becomes Truth, which is oneness.

A person who has completely died
and returned to the place before human minds -
a person who has become the one God -
has everything and knows everything;
he is omnipotent and omniscient.

It is not possible to go to heaven or be reborn in heaven
without going through the true Buddha within oneself.
Nor can one live forever.
Because he is not Truth, he does not live forever -
he does not exist.

Only oneness is true,
only oneness saves people,
only oneness truly gives salvation,
only oneness can be resurrected.

A person who is Truth and oneness must appear,
for only he can give salvation.
No one can get to heaven
without going through this oneness.
When one returns to heaven and earth
and becomes Buddha, the originally existing entity,
heaven and earth are within him,
and he exists within heaven and earth.

Such a person can give salvation because he is oneness itself.
Heaven and earth will live according to man's will,
as will all people.
Only man can save heaven, earth, and man.

By man's will,
heaven, earth, and man will live.
Heaven and all things exist
when man is Truth and oneness.
When people live like me,
as me;
when they live for all people becoming one,
so that all may be born in heaven;
it is then that it will become a world
where all live as one.

Such a place is not here, there,
or in some other place - heaven cannot be seen with human eyes.
The place where all things live is where they have been reborn
inside my complete consciousness.

When I die, I am reborn,
and when I die, I become Truth.

The time of all things living in the complete land of God,
is now.

One's life

I f a person asks what life is,
I answer that there is no Truth in life.

If someone insists life is Truth,
I tell him his burden is heavy.

If he says that life is fun,
I tell him he is dreaming a fun dream.

If he complains of life being weary,
I tell him to lay down his useless greed.

If he speaks of the futility of life,
I tell him neither life nor death exists.

If he declares that life is wrong,
I tell him he has greed and attachments to life.

If he says life is fragrant,
I tell him he is near the world of Truth,

and if he says he is scared of life,
I tell him that he is living his life well.

If he asserts life is suffering,
I tell him to eliminate himself,

and if he says that life is happiness,
I tell him that it is but a bubble.

If someone asks how to live life well,
I tell him to live a life completely without self.

If he asks what kind of life is true,
I tell him that a true life is one that Truth lives -
such a life is Truth itself.

If he asks how to make his life a true one,
I tell him I hold that key.

Cradle

U nable to feed her children,
she clutched her empty stomach and sighed;
she lay awake all night worrying about feeding them.
Such were our mothers.

She did not scold those little urchins,
who wet themselves in the middle of the night
while sleeping in their mother's arms.
Instead she shivered all night in her damp clothes,
then dried them
while preparing breakfast in the morning.
Such were our mothers.

There was so much work to be done in the fields
that she could not hear her children crying of hunger.
They cried themselves to exhaustion,
but she did not know.

Some fell ill and died, leaving their parents much agony
as they buried their children in the mountains.

As a child, I had cotton clothes to wear;
thus I did not look like a savage.
However this did not prevent my life from being primitive,
as times were very hard.

The country was stripped of itself after Japanese colonial rule,
and soon after there was war.
It was during this time that I was born.
My family was in dire poverty; in fact every family was.
Every family had at least six, seven, eight, or even nine children;
in fact every tenant farming family did.
We would go to gather wood in the mountains
where there were human bones and bullets
scattered everywhere.
Parents went out into the fields
leaving behind their babies at home.
They cried and cried in hunger
and resorted to picking up and eating chicken droppings and
even their own feces.
They became exhausted
and slept on the bare ground in the yard.

Sometimes they tumbled from the room onto the dirt floors of
their houses, which in the countryside were quite high.
They would tumble down onto the dirt floor
and then would tumble down into the yard,
but even though they took such hard falls,
they never got hurt.
Perhaps it was Providence.

After having worked all day,
the mother finally returned home to suckle her baby.
The sound of him gulping the milk down was like
the gurgle of water going down a drain.
His eyes filled with happiness,
his face smudged all over with dirt.
His tears finally dried as he fondled his mother's breasts.

Senility was a disease that many developed with old age.
Many lost their consciousness as they became older.
It was a disease that was caused by frequent starvation.
In fact, there were many who died of it.
There were those who were sick
but were too poor to go to the hospital;
they eventually passed away at home, staring at the ceiling.
When I was a child,

I had many friends who were pockmarked by disease.

Even my older brothers had come down with smallpox.

We had been too poor

and could do nothing but look to the sky:

they eventually died.

According to the neighbors,

my mother had wailed madly, beating her fists into the ground.

After my brothers' departures,

I was born into the world as the precious son.

In my village,

it was customary to give a child a humble name,

for people believed that the child would then be healthy

and not die.

Thus as a child, my name was *Gah-jee*,

short for *gang-ah-jee*, meaning puppy.

In fact,

there were many children named Gah-jee in my village.

The kids would make fun of my name,

and so growing up, I hated hearing it.

At the age of six,

I began the chore of gathering grass for the cows

and feeding them.

I would feed them, then come home with a bushel of grass
to make boiled cattle feed.
My sister was not allowed to go to school but I was.
Sometime when I was in
the lower grades of elementary school,
I was out on the hill behind my school
drawing a picture
when my sister called out to me, "Gah-jee!"
After arriving home, I hit my sister.

In first grade,
my class went on a school field trip to a reservoir;
it was an eight kilometer walk to get there.
Seeing as I had travelled such a long distance,
my mother had come out to the road
to greet me and take me home upon my return.
She had my youngest sibling strapped onto her back,
but still she carried me home.
My mother will turn eighty next year.
To her, I will always be her precious son.
In fact when I was in the third grade
she bought me a little desk.
I was so fond of that desk, and I studied at it whenever I could.
Many things occurred while I was in the third grade:

my older sister got married and left our home;

a few days later after her marriage,

my father visited her and her in-laws.

My father had been working at a train station

up north in Nanam

when a tree fell on him.

He was badly injured but eventually recovered.

However, later on his illness returned

and this led him to his death.

At the time,

my father's friends held me in their arms and cried endlessly.

After my father had passed away,

I had to act as the head of the family from a very young age.

My mother fashioned a wooden A-frame carrier,

or a *jee-gae,* for me to carry on my back.

After school,

I would come home and take that jee-gae with me

to work in the fields

and to gather wood from the mountains;

so diligent was I!

During the three years that followed after his death,

we held memorial ceremonies, or *jae-sa,* for my father:

every first and fifteenth day of the month

we would lament at his memorial altar in our house,
and once a year we would slaughter a pig as an offering.
With ceaseless envy,
I would look upon the other kids
playing out in the schoolyard.
I would take off my shoes and walk barefoot
in the mountains and the fields
lest my shoes become worn.
The marriages of all three of my older sisters
and the jae-sa for my father
left our family in needy circumstances.
Indeed I grew up with much heartache and sorrow.

The poor country folk all went abroad.
Without any footing, they left their homes
and so they faced many hardships.
But now they are the ones
who are the leaders of the world.

Green Mountains

In the days
when there were not many people living in the world,
every mountain was green.

The green mountains that people speak of
are the ones in which the trees are lustrous with green.
But the green mountains of Truth are not those -
green mountains and bald mountains are the same.

The term 'green mountains' is one that man has made;
an enlightened person deems them to be non-existent.
The green mountains of the Mind are pure as pure can be,
but it is invisible in the eyes of man.

When will man be able to find the green mountains?

Slash-and-Burn farmer

He who makes his living off of
cultivating fields in the mountains
searches far and wide into its rough depths.
He will farm the land for consecutive years
until the soil becomes infertile.

He is a father;
after having cultivated the land for a few months alone,
he brings his family there
and they toil the new land together.
There they build a new hut for themselves
and live together as a family.

Wild boars, deer, and pheasants come and eat the grains.
These families live together with the creatures of the mountains.
They place a large rock propped up with a wooden plank,
and beneath it they put some grains;

when a boar trips the prop stick,

the rock falls and the boar is crushed underneath.

Many a day had passed without any meat on the table,

but now they are able to feast for days.

The nearest town is twenty kilometers

or perhaps forty kilometers away;

the children walk the narrow mountain roads with

lightening speed.

They plant potatoes, sweet potatoes, and corn,

which are their staple foods.

These are people who eat the wild greens

that they gather from the mountains.

They are simple-hearted people

for they have no expectations;

with their pure hearts, they live with Nature.

They have nothing and so they want nothing.

They just live observing the sky and the earth;

if they were to be greedy,

it would be that they want the sky to send them rain.

But there are those who grow tired of this kind of life.

So they come to the city,

only to find that they can do nothing else

but undertake manual labor jobs for they are uneducated.

They become unhappy

and they come to miss the warmth of the bygone days;

they blame the city and its lack of warmth.

Though people long for a love in which

there exists no distance between them,

people use it, which is why there is no love at all.

The cultivated fields are all disappearing;

the homes that were built beyond the slopes

and the homes that lined the valleys

have all become abandoned.

How many years have passed, no one knows,

but the land has become thick with weeds.

Those who used to live off the mountains

have all gone far away to make money.

It is a pity that those people have become hardened

and have lost their warmth

Pravrajyā

You fool!
What is the point in you becoming Buddha all alone?
You are abandoning

your parents,

your wife,

and your children!" she says to him.

Yet he tears himself away from his elderly mother.

His wife cries silently without a word.

Although he is leaving,

his mind is full of burdens - his sins -

and he knows not where to go.

Due to their ties,

his family awaits his return anxiously.

Every time the front gate squeaks,

they check to see if he has returned.

At home things change with the years,

but he is deep in the mountains seeking enlightenment.

After a while, he may think he has reached it,

but he has gained no insight,

just like the numerous high priests

who have all passed away

without being able to save mankind.

In the perfect world,

one would have a family while on his path to seek Truth;

only then would that truly be the act of saving mankind.

Now it is time for him - for everyone -

to come down from the mountain

and have a family,

just as he has always wanted.

There is no need for one to undergo such an ascetic life,

for now are the days in which

man may become Truth naturally.

Thus let us take part in such times.

Memories

U pon the windy hills you lay
thinking about memories past,
which bring tears to your eyes
and a sigh to your breath.
No one asks you why;
you are alone,
watching the woolly clouds
float lightly across the sky.
As you look to the sky,
you feel as if
there is something missing -
something that seems just out of reach -
but a something that you want to find.

All you do is sigh as you look back upon your life
which has been riddled with pointless sadness.
Indeed they say that life is like floating duckweed,

but having to live it in this manner is such a shame.
You know nothing,
which is why you have been able to accomplish nothing
throughout the years that have passed.
Upon seeing those dear to you disperse,
all you can do is cry.

Everything is existent and non-existent in the Universe.
Everything that is existent in the Universe is as it is,
but man lives thinking that
there is something beyond the Universe.

Grieve as you may to Nature over the fact that
human life is a useless thing
and that it is all just a dream,
Nature remains silent.
When you are removed from human life
and then look back on it,
the days in which you lived a human-bound life
will be a distant dream.

Mother, sister

M other, sister,
listen to my words,
for something miraculous has happened.
I, who knew nothing
and lived an immature life,
am now doing the work of heaven.

I was neither bad nor good,
and my destiny was always to live a difficult life
doing what others do not.
I lived that life, simply accepting it
because it is the will of heaven.
It was my destiny.

All those who left sighs of regret behind them
and went in search of Truth,
they must have had these same feelings,

these feelings, these minds,
of having to leave home and bid the world farewell.
The world of heaven
is the world where I now live,
and in order to teach people of this world,
I am leaving home;
I am leaving home.

I do not have any regrets or sadness,
or indeed any minds at all,
but now that my human mind has changed
and I have become a person of heaven,
now that my human habits are gone
and I am a person of heaven,
tears are flowing down my face
and I do not know
whether they are tears of sadness or joy.

Mother, sister, I am in my land.
I, who had the most childish mind,
have built a house in heaven,
and here in the new heaven
I have become a master,
Mother, sister, I have become a king.

In human years, I am now nearly an old man,
but my mind still seeks you, mother and sister, like a child.
Why am I so like a child?
There is no one to listen to my woes;
I have no choice but to tell the messages of my heart
to you - my mother and sister.

Life flows by like water,
and with it, you aged.
My woes and complaints are simply the minds from my
childhood,
and mother, sister, you listened to them all.
Now, there is no one to talk to or lean on.

Saving people is something that I must do,
even if I have to beg -
I must do it, no matter what happens.
It is something I must do
regardless of the obstacles and sufferings that befall me.

But mother, sister, do not worry;
I can tell all people
that I have become a king,
and I can make them my people.

How joyous is this,
and what an honor!
But mother, sister, when I look back,
I have a wife and children
from my life as a human being.
If I have any worries at all,
it is that I worry about how they will live
when I do this work.

I was simply living life as a man,
searching for Truth, perhaps a little more diligently than others,
and I became enlightened through a serendipitous opportunity.
I now know that I am none other than the person who must
deliver
the news of heaven,
but I lived as other people did,
devoting my whole body to that life.

Now that life has taken a backseat.
I only do the work of heaven,
but just as when I lived in the human world,
I will devote everything I have.

My wish is like a children's poem,

and it is to live always with you, mother and sister.

But now I work as a person of the people,

as someone who has left everything -

my mother, sister, wife, and children.

In the past I lived with ties made in the world,

but now I am going back to my place in the origin.

My human mind wishes for you,

mother, sister, and all of your children,

to come to my wonderful world,

but you still see me as only a young boy.

So I go to my land without telling you.

As a person that belongs to the world,

I go to protect it.

If perhaps we should meet again later,

come to my land.

Let's live there together.

Let's live there forever.

If we were not able to live as we dreamt,

with affection in the human world,

it was simply because making a living took all of our time.

With that dream left unfulfilled,

again, I leave.

Wandering

A person who chases floating clouds
knows many things, but he is too lazy to do farm work.
People who chase floating clouds
are arrogant despite the criticisms of those around them,
and they waste away their parents' fortune.
This is why they are called educated loafers.
With great ambitions but no jobs,
the world does not go according to their will.

They run around town selling the land they have,
but they do not accomplish anything,
so they simply lose the land.
When they return to their hometowns
because there is nowhere else for them to go,
no one welcomes them back.
They go and gamble
in an effort to regain what they had,

but their wealth shrinks further,
and left with nothing
they walk tipsily with a bottle in hand.

During Japanese colonial rule,
our poor neighbors left their homes
to go and earn money in the cities, or to Japan,
and some even went to Bongchun in Manchuria
and became dog traders.
They dreamed of returning when they earned enough money
and worked hard to gain a foothold there,
but by the time they had earned enough to stop worrying,
their hair had already turned grey.

When they do return,
the hometown they dreamed of no longer exists.
All the people they knew have gone somewhere,
with strangers in their places,
and with indescribable regret,
they make their way back.
Those who went North, to Manchuria, to Russia,
or even further abroad, are unable to return
because of their circumstances.
Even if they do return, a time of sorrow awaits them

for their parents and siblings they dreamed of seeing again
are no longer there.
The mind does not age, so they may believe their parents
they saw in the past might still be alive,
but they are not there when they arrive
and they lose the refuge of their minds.
Their hometowns are like a foreign place.

In the human world,
everyone desires to eat and live well,
but we live lives of scrimping and saving,
and raising the children with nothing.
These were our lives.
Those who were disgruntled by this
looked for an easy way out;
they sold the farm and land,
and looked for gold beneath rainbows,
but for certain
their days would have been filled with sighs of regret.

There are so many who left their homes for the cities.
How much must they have suffered,
that so many of them never return.
Now for everyone,

where they currently live are their homes,
but they still hold onto their hometowns in their minds.
It is not people's human minds, but their true minds
that miss their hometowns.
They miss the time when they lived there
because it is where they came from,
and it is a place of refuge and rest.
Even if it was a time when food was scarce,
it was a time when they lived with their mothers.

A person misses this time even more
when he has no one to lean on.
But more than that, it is the thought of his parents,
unaware of time passing while waiting for him,
weeping every time the cherry blossoms in the yard bloomed
reminding them of him and when he left.
The thought of them makes him blink back tears.

Those who were dragged to the army
unaware of life and death;
those split from us as our nation split into North and South;
this is the sorrow of our nation.
We must unite
so that we can once more live together as one.

We were split because of our own greed,

which is why we have many regrets and sorrows

and lived in such poverty.

This is the reason many left for foreign lands,

leaving behind their wives and children.

When they returned home after growing old,

their hometowns themselves have become a foreign place,

their once young wives, grandmothers,

and their babies, middle-aged adults.

After living abroad,

perhaps with a wife and children,

when one returns to his hometown,

he is disappointed.

Once he returns, he finds

his years of regret and poverty have become sin.

They have become sorrow.

Who is there to blame?

People must live the years of sorrow

with a united will and without sorrows and regrets.

A united world must come

in order for regrets and sorrows to disappear.

Hiking

Hiking is climbing up a mountain - this is what hiking is.
The reason hiking is so good for you is
the clear water and clean air,
and the joy that comes from the mountains, water, and nature.

Hiking is good because it makes you move every part of your body,
even the very marrow of your bones.
Hiking is good because it makes a person
reflect back on himself.
Hiking is good because after suffering,
it makes him let go of all that he was wrestling with.
Hiking is good because one can learn
the balance and harmony of nature.
Hiking is good because with nature,
one can shed what he has been tainted with.
Hiking is good because the sense of achievement
gives one's body and mind joy.

Hiking is good because for a moment,

he does not have greed.

Man tried to find innocence amidst his many, many thoughts

while climbing the mountains,

but it was impossible because of his present reality

which have deep roots that lie hidden.

He can do what is best for his body, for himself,

but this is far from the path of finding his true self.

People do not know the movement and survival of all things

are dependent on the management of Truth.

A calling

How pretty the girl with long hair looked,
when she ran with a smile upon her face
to a safe place that nobody knows;
how beautiful she looked.
The girl with the bob,
the girl with the braided hair,
the girl with the parting -
they were all beautiful,
and they all had many beautiful dreams
and they were all far better off than I.

My heart fluttered when I saw them,
and even though I wanted to talk to them,
I was only able to blush.
Those girls in their black uniforms and bulky school-bags,
have now become middle-aged.
In my youth, I could not date anyone

because studying and making a living
kept me more than busy.
Man desires something
when it is the time - at such a time he comes to have such
emotions.
This was my adolescence
and it is the providence of God.

Man experiences all sorts of things in his life,
many kinds of troubles,
so he should know better,
but he remains ignorant
because he has minds inside his mind.
Though the people of the world
may have had their beautiful time of dreams and hopes,
it is called life because even after they grow old
they still live with hope.
Without hope,
no one is of any worth.
People live with hope until they grow old and die.
I am at an age that is neither old nor young,
and now I use my experiences to save people.
This job is the best job of all that you can have for a lifetime,
and it has been given to me, and I save people.

I live having forgotten
the regrets and sighs with which I lived,
and because I have neither maturity nor any minds,
it is the only duty I have.

I have been assigned the work of heaven,
and I worry whether I will act like a person in charge of heaven's
work.
It is said that when heaven creates such a person,
only a person of use will be created,
but it makes me think that I am not such a person,
and that I am not enough for the job
because in life, I was neither noble nor base.

Nostalgia

Over in the far hills,
the herders are sleeping,
oblivious of where the cows have gone.
Those who just sleep,
do not know where the cows have gone,
and when they wake up,
they find that they are old and weak,
and have spent the years dreaming a sad dream,
a futile dream.
Why is life,
why are people,
so sad and feeble?
It is pitiful.
No one knows.
There is no one that knows.
They waste their youth,
spending it dreaming useless dreams;

they waste away their good years.

I want to go,
I want to go to the endless horizon where there is nothing but
grass,
stretching out endlessly, further than the eye can see.
I want to roll and run there like a colt,
shrugging off worries, anxieties, this, that, and everything.
My hometown is no different than my mind at a time
when I would run and play in the fields
near the mountain graveyards of my home.
I was a young child,
a mischievous, immature child.
I did not have a lot to eat,
but neither did I starve.
All that I want
is a place of rest.

The human mind

People like shallow gambits and artifices.
People like guile and cunning.

People like to coddle their bodies.

People like to boast about themselves.

People like to save face.

People like to protect themselves.

People like their attachments.

People like wealth.

People like to boast and brag.

People like to show off their shallow knowledge.

People like liquor and sex.

People like not having to move their bodies.

People like talking the talk, but not walking the walk.

People like to live however they please.

People like envying others.

People like it when things work out for themselves.

People like it when things work out for their families.

People like advancing and succeeding.

People like longing for something.

People like being acknowledged by others.

People like to put on airs.

People like looking down on others.

People like to dream useless and vain dreams.

People like to ignore and flout heaven.

Words

W ords are one's mind;
There are words that are one's own
and there are words of the Universe.
When words are spoken well,
it can have a great impact on the listener;
but when they are not, they cause much distress.
In a world full of words, false and useless words cannot even be
called words.
True words are those that are spoken with no self whatsoever.
One must always speak sincerely for sincerity is Truth -
always speak words that are calm and peaceful;
always speak words without mind;
always speak with a constant heart;
always speak words that can be kept;
always speak your own mind;
always speak your will without any mind;
always speak carefully;

always speak of things just as they are;

always think before speaking;

always speak in a bright manner;

always speak affectionately;

always speak politely;

always speak like an innocent wife;

always speak cheerfully, in a pleasing tone;

always speak from the other person's point of view;

always speak from the heart;

always speak with warm affection;

always speak in a way that benefits the listener.

Only when one always speaks in this way

are his words those of value and Truth.

Returning home

Let us return home,
to the home that is yours and mine.
Our home is in this heaven and earth
but neither you nor I knew,
and we tried to find it in a faraway place.

Let us return home,
to the home that is yours and mine.
Where is that home that no one could find?
It is not anywhere but here.

There is a great commotion to find what is right next to them,
I find it pathetic.
I find it a shame and a pity.
People are that way because they live bound
to the words of saints in a faraway place.
The greatest saint is he who has found himself.

What is it that you are trying to know
when you have not even found yourself?
What are you trying to find,
when your home is your very self?
Do not search for it in physical form,
there is no difference between home and grave.
The grave is your home.

Calmness

C almness is to be the same.
Calmness has no hierarchy.

Calmness is togetherness, and it has no airs.

Calmness is to be same on the inside as the outside.

When there is calmness, no one lives in poverty.

Calmness includes all people.

Calmness is nature's flow.

In calmness, there are no conditions.

In calmness, there is no one who is superior or inferior.

In calmness, all people live good lives.

Calmness is to become one with others.

Calmness is not a life lived how one pleases.

Calmness is a life lived for others.

In calmness, there is no boasting.

In calmness, there is no gossip and rumors.

In calmness, there may be discontent, but it abates quickly,

and calmness is the unification of the whole.

Calmness is to live well.

Penance

A hunter is gasping for breath;
no one knows whether those who run
are gasping for breath or struggling.

Everything is self-centered,
and it is because I exist that I gasp for breath.

Man is an existence who does not know -
A human being is an existence who does not know -

It does not matter whether creations struggle,
or whether they live or die if he does not exist.

When he does something without self,
he is not affected by the struggle.
When he does something without self,
he does not know this or that.

Life

A man on a path halts and hesitates;
he looks tired, weary from walking.
The man on the path continues and hurries onwards
but even if he reaches his destination,
there is nothing for him to gain.

It makes no difference whether or not he achieves his end,
but ignorant of heaven's will, all he does is sigh.
Just as a refugee longs for home;
just as a nursing baby longs for his mother;
all people live dreaming of an ideal world.
They may even believe that
the ideal world exists in the dream,
but though they long for it
like a refugee or a nursing baby,
I hold the key to that world.
Although life has homesickness,

since man can neither see it nor find it,
heaven has come to show him.

All creations, all things, are silent when they come into the world,
and they leave it just as silently,
Where have the heroes of the past gone?
Only stories of them handed down through the years remain.

People live within time,
but they are fooled by the moment,
and repeatedly live lives that do not remain.
And yet, they claim to be clever.

It is life and it is all creations -
those who talk and brag,
the miserly and the great -
they all eventually turn silent
and disappear.

Salvation

There are many, so many people struggling while living;
    in life, all people are wanderers from birth.
Living in the world is suffering
and all people suffer and are burdened.
But no one knows this,
and all anyone can see are their own troubles.

Though there may be heart-breaking events
and one may live wanting to die,
time cures everything; it erases that heartache.
One may think that there cannot possibly be more pain
than what he is experiencing,
but it is something that passes,
and something all wanderers must face.

Do not cry with sorrow, but come to me.

Do not wail with sorrow, and come to me.
There is no one else who can lighten your load
and bear your burden.

There are hundreds of different kinds of heartache;
if you are sobbing because you have lost a loved one,
I will find him for you.
If you are mourning the death of a loved one,
I will find him for you.
I will teach you that life and death do not exist.

If you want to die because you have lost your wealth,
I will give you a greater prize than that fortune.
If you have been betrayed by someone, a friend, or lover,
I will give you something better.

If you are awaiting the return of someone who left without a
word, I will guide you to a place that is better than that person.
All people with heartbreak and sorrow, come -
I will bear all of your burdens,
so do not hesitate, and come find me.

Regret

A sick man lies down in a frosty-cold room,
and thinking back over the years
tears run down his face.
Not knowing where it is he should go,
or where he has come from,
his fate has been to live a life of struggle,
and he has become ill, to boot.

His wife, who despite their scarce means
served him like a god, is now buried and gone,
and tears blur his sight as he thinks of her.
He wonders when his son will come back
from serving in the army; his days of youth,
when he was just married, seem like yesterday,
but an endless amount of time has gone by.
Frustration and desolation
keep the tears falling.

When he was young, he lived with his family,
together with his affectionate parents.
But now that he is old and weak,
his siblings in the next village do not visit him once.
Deep at night, he is alone in an empty room,
waiting endlessly.
It is his fate to die alone, and having become such
he knows that life was in vain.

Since he is still holding onto his last breath,
his neighbors take pity on him and give him a bowl of porridge.
What is life, and what is it to have lived?
There is no use in regretting a futile life,
but his tears keep falling as he thinks of his past self
which he can never return to.
He is not an educated man,
but if he could leave behind something in the world,
it is that people should live with compassion
while they are still in the world.
No one listens.

He keeps his mouth shut;
he has lived seeking God,
he has lived committing many sins and many wrongs,

and a few days after repenting,

he passes away.

Relatives come in droves

and bury him in the ground.

He leaves life, still holding onto many regrets and sorrows,

and since he has learned nothing,

he does not know where to go.

Steeped in the habits of life,

he has only made scraps of his mind.

He is the same as when he was living,

and he does not know who he is.

He continues as he is, not knowing that he is dead,

and since he died without wisdom,

he is unable to become enlightened.

He keeps wandering and wandering -

when will he be able to find his true self?

My name

I n winter, the strong winds in the hills feel heartless,
but the wind in the summer hills arouses gratitude.
The wind always blows,
but people judge the wind.
The wind is something that neither comes nor goes,
but people judge it because they do not know.
Not knowing what life is, and what it is to live,
they are greedy.

Children who cried of hunger in a poverty stricken Korea
are now the leaders, the driving force, of the world.
They struggle, in order that they may never go hungry again.
People live immaturely, purely to survive,
but I wish for people to live knowing Truth.
Do not bury Truth in your heart,
but live diligently.
What good is there

in living only for yourself?

What good can come of caring only for yourself?

I see the lives that you live,

and they are so filled with greed.

You live looking down on others

with your greed for money,

but to me, it seems absurd.

When you die, as all of us will,

will you be able to take that money with you?

When you die, as we all will,

what need will you have for money?

I too was born with nothing,

and I tried my best to live as other people do.

This blasted world of money,

in it, one is a fool without it,

and without it, he cannot do anything;

it is dumbfounding.

Money is that which bruises people's hearts.

I worked hard,

twice as hard as other people;

I really worked hard.

What I wanted was to live like a human being should -

a life of calmness and peace.
Those who flattered government officials,
and those who used government money,
could spend money;
people without power could not see a penny.
How many people who were too poor to go to the hospital
died in their homes?
The rich may be happy
taking advantage of the less fortunate,
but they leave heartache in their wake.

It was not easy to live a human life;
it was no easy feat to raise kids
and support a wife.
Although it was not easy to live, I sought Truth.
After I became enlightened,
the affairs of the world are my will.
The life I lived as a human being
was endlessly futile.
When I was young, many people became pock-marked
from small pox, and many people died.
Stricken with poverty,
many people died.
The old hungered and died senile - these were the common

circumstances of my village when I was young.

My elementary school was close to home,

so I would go to school barefooted.

My nickname was Puppy.

Children were often given this nickname,

because they kept dying.

It was said that if they were given humble names,

death would pass over them.

Why did I hate this childhood nickname so much?

I often lost my temper

when people called me Puppy.

Both of my older brothers suffered from smallpox

and passed away,

so Puppy was my name until I grew up.

It was my name.

Magician

I f something came forth
from the sky that is so far away,
what would it be?
The whole Universe is a Soul,
and when there is soil and water,
and when the temperature and humidity are just right,
anything can be made.
This is what a magician is;
it is a true magician.
Everything is made from this place,
from all living things that are made as perfection,
to microscopic organisms.
How strange and wondrous it is!

Lacking nothing, wanting for nothing,
it is that which simply exists in that place.
The form and the quality is the same;

the former is not visible to human eyes and the latter is, therefore,

people live without knowing where they come from.

People try to find answers
in human thought,
but it is something that cannot be known
in this way.
This complete entity which lacks nothing,
simply comes into existence and disappears.

What is it that the forms of all things have?
They all have lifespans
all things have lifespans
and to have a lifespan means it is finite.
What is it to be finite?
It is to have limits,
which determines its end.

All creations come from earth, water, wind, and fire,
they live as earth, water, wind, and fire,
and return to earth, water, wind, and fire.
Why do we age?
Earth, water, wind, and fire make people age.

It is the balance and harmony of heaven and earth

that was not made this or that way by anyone;

As the phrase "balance and harmony of heaven and earth"

indicates,

the place that comes and goes, of and by itself,

is neither existence nor non-existence;

it is the substance of the master of the Universe.

Looking at the world with my eyes closed,

everything in the world

is all within me.

Looking at the world with my eyes open,

that world is right here.

Foolish people,

foolish, foolish people -

even though they have it all,

they do not know that they do.

If they open their eyes and see,

they will know that their real substance is the Universe as it is,

and it is only themselves that do not exist.

Heaven

Time does not pass in heaven;
in heaven, time does not exist.
It is a pure place,
a beautiful place.

If the people of the world
all come to this heaven,
worries or woes
would not exist.

It is the place of life,
it is a place where all creations exist.
Let us all abide by nature's flow,
and go to this place.

The Universe's Mind

The radiant sun shines
without discriminating between
the rich and poor, or the high and low.

Look at the sun -
does it distinguish between this and that?
does it shine differently for the rich as it does for the poor?

Everything done by the Universe
is the same as the sun -
there are no gaps or gulfs at all.

It is because you do not know
and it is because you are immature
that you believe without any knowledge -
but know that all such things are in vain.
Look at me,

I exist forever, yesterday and today,
as well as in the distant future.

My true self is not confined,
my true self does not belong to anything.
Be enlightened of my land, where I neither die nor live.

There is no one who is great
and there is no one who is inferior.
Everyone in the world is
the same.

It is people that give heartache and pain;
people who think they are great,
it is human to believe that greatness
is knowing many lies.

To all brothers and sisters!
All, all hold hands,
come to the land of heaven, and come into my arms.
My land is without any human suffering;
it is where there are no days of cold winds blowing;
where there are no people crying of hunger.
What is the most fulfilling thing in the world?

It is going to the land of heaven;
you may have heard of the land of God,
but those who receive my teachings
will know where that land is.

In the future, when my words spread to the ends of the world,
and all people believe,
there may come a day when
people sympathize with my current state,
that there is no one believing in my words today.

I know Truth,
and I am trying to teach you
because you are immature and you do not know Truth at all -
that is all.

In a sorrowful world,
we all lived human lives together,
but the difference was whether one knew or was ignorant.
Having come from heaven
the work that I must do,
is to live among you and guide you to my land.

It is to teach you my love,

and how to live in the world
according to the natural order of the Universe.
What is it to live well,
and what is it to live poorly?
No one is equal, which is why this work exists.

I will teach you if you are wrong,
I will guide you when you stumble;
and should you sigh from regrets,
let us share those sighs together.
I am the master of heaven,
but people do not know this,
not even those who seek Truth.
No one,
not a single person knows that I am of the highest.
They simply see me as another human being,
and pass on by.
This is what immaturity is -
a world that asks me to prove what I am.

The world is one that demands proof,
one that demands evidence.
It is a world that asks why
because it is a world that has lost trust in everything.

Truth does not exist in falseness,
Truth does not exist in pretence.
True words are no longer true,
because the world is in an aftermath of
falseness parading as Truth.

If you are to know the form and traits of heaven,
if you are to know the will of heaven,
you can know, you can all know,
when your selves do not exist.

You are so covered in dirt, you are unable to recognize me,
and you are so covered in dirt, you cannot even see me.
You may be covered in many layers of dirt,
but I have come to scrub your dirt away.
I am no ordinary dirt-scrubber -
I am complete and perfect.
There is nowhere that I cannot scrub,
and when you shed that dirt,
you can come to my world.
Your dirt must be scrubbed away,
in order for you to come to my land.

A Talk with a Star

- It is good to see you, star!

  Star: I am very happy to see you!

- Star, when were you created?

  Star: I was created a long, long time ago.

- Have many people come and gone from the world?

  Star: Yes. Many, many people have come and gone.

- Star, why were you born?

  Star: I was not born; I simply exist as I am.

- Star, you truly know a lot. Do you have any complaints?

  Star: Yes, I do. People see me simply as a star.

- How should they see you?

  Star: I am a star, but I have already departed from being a star.

- Oh, you truly know a lot! Are you me?

  Star: Yes, I am.

- How were you enlightened of that?

  Star: I came to know on my own during a long period of time.

- Star, Buddha became enlightened when he saw you - what
  does that mean?

Star: Even though I existed as I was, it was his mind that distinguished existence and non-existence of form. Then he realized on his own that to be with or without form is the same.

- Star, explain it more simply so that others can understand. Star: When Buddha saw the sky, I existed amidst nothingness. He saw me and realized that what shape is and shapeless is, and that both are the same. Buddha knew that originally I was without a shape but changed to a shape.

- Star, to what extent have I been enlightened? Star: You are completely without self, and you alone in the world have reached the state of enlightenment. Though you live life, you are not bound to it; you love but you are not in it; you yearn and yet you are not bound by yearning; you curse but you are not bound by cursing. You have departed from all things so you are the highest and ultimate pioneer of Truth, for the first time in the history of the Universe.

- Star, do you even know such things? Star: Yes, I do. I was recently enlightened of these things, and gained great freedom. I do not dwell in my form, though I have form; and my form exists amidst nothingness, and amidst existence all things exist, so all things are just as they are.

- Star, let's talk again another time. You truly know my heart. You and I are one.

A Talk with the Blue Sky

- Blue sky, thank you for your hard work.

  Blue sky: Not at all. I am simply doing my work. I am you, the master, and aren't you me?

- There is no place in which the sky does not exist. Though the sky is me, no one knows this. People search for heaven, expecting it to be in the shapes they imagine. The blue sky remains silent and just stares absent-mindedly at the futile human life. Blue sky, are you neither cold nor hot?

  Blue sky: Cold and hot no longer exist for me, nor anything at all. They simply just exist.

- Blue sky, is it true that you create all form through your movement?

  Blue sky: Yes, it is so. When I move, all forms are created from within me, and they disappear into me. Although what is within me is invisible, it lacks nothing.

A Talk with the Sun

- Sun, it is good to see you!

  Sun: It is good to see you! Master, it is really good to see you. You have finally come to Earth! During my life as a sun, I have never seen something live as vilely and chaotically as people.

- How can things become peaceful?

  Sun: Now that you are here, things will become peaceful.

- What do you desire?

  Sun: I do not desire anything. I simply like existing as you made me.

- How long will you live?

  Sun: I will live as long as you order me to live.

A Talk with the Moon

- The moon is whispering to me when I look up in the sky.
  Moon: It is good to see you!
- Yes. Thank you for keeping your place in the blue sky. Moon,
  what would you like to do?
  Moon: I would like to go to you, master.
- When you have finished your duty and you die in the far
  distant future, I will allow you to come to me.
  Moon: Thank you. I really dislike being tied to this form.
  Thank you so much!
- Moon, you may cry. Are you happy?
  Moon: Yes.

A Talk with a Mountain

- Mountain, good to see you!

  Mountain: It is really good to see you!

- Is your life interesting?

  Mountain: No. I do not find it interesting.

- When were you created?

  Mountain: A long, long time ago, a ball of fire eventually became me, a mountain.

- What would you like to become?

  Mountain: I would like to become water.

- Why is that?

  Mountain: Because if I become water, I would be able to flow as water does.

- You and water are one and the same.

  Mountain: How can I be the same as water?

- It is a shame that you do not know.

The way to finding the true path and enlightenment

L ies have become Truth because people are fooled by
religion, fooled by books,
fooled and fooled again by people.
No one knew Truth, and it remained buried.
Now, it has come to the world by the Universe's natural order.
Truth has been awaited by all religions.
Having come to know it,
this person has become the master of the world.
No matter how intelligent a person is,
he is just a fool if he does not know Truth,
but if a fool knows Truth, he is a complete and perfect saint.
What is true is none other than Truth,
what is true does not change, and what is true lives forever.

People are insecure because all current religions, societies,
politics, and cultures are not righteous.
One realizes that everything is false when he knows Truth,
one can become a saint when he knows Truth.
In life and in death, Truth lives in the land of God.

There was no one who could teach Truth,
but now true heaven has come to Earth.

In order to go to the true world of Truth,
one must cleanse his mind and find his true self, the Universe.
This is the level of enlightenment that Shakyamuni reached,
but now in the complete world,
when one is completely enlightened, he can meet God,
and confirm that he lives forever in the world of God.

If one cleanses his mind and gets the state of enlightenment,
he receives the ability to save people.
Saints will come forth in droves
and they will go to every corner of the world.
This *dō*, this practice, is completion,
that was awaited by each religion for thousands of years.
The chance for anyone to become a saint has finally come.
Man lives a life that is limited in time,
so there is eternally no way to be compensated for
his wrongful life if he is bound and attached to his religion.
Heaven sends forth saints in the hour of need.
The real chance to gain complete enlightenment
has finally come, now -
do not hesitate to find the path, the *dō*, of true Truth.

Conclusion

Mind is the entire universe. It is Buddha, Holy Father and Holy Spirit, the body and the mind of the universe, and the emptiness and the consciousness.

However, as humans live, they have karma and habit in their lives, and therefore cannot see Truth. I write this book to make people discard their lives, which is the karma, and their bodies, which are the habit, and so have Truth.

When one discards his mind, which is karma, and rids the body, which is habit, the world is Heaven and he will live forever. The world where one dies and is reborn is Heaven. It is the world where all are one. When all become one which is the origin, then all are Truth which is one. All will be reborn and live. Life and death are the same as one. One will realize that the true existence can live by the law of existing and non-existing.

When I close my eyes, the entire universe is the emptiness and the consciousness, the body of Buddha and the mind of Buddha, Holy Spirit and Holy Father, and the body and the mind of the universe. All are one; they are God originally. Since everything is reborn as God, all beings are God. The law of life is that only the clean ones who cleansed their mind can be born. In Buddhism, the Sutras say to empty one's mind. In Christianity, the Bible says those whose mind is poor can go to Heaven. People can understand these sayings when they know the identity of the mind, and empty it.

All beings are one, and all beings are Truth. One whose mind is cleansed can see God and Buddha. Salvation of what exists is the last act of Truth. It is what Truth can do and does.

Everything lives as it is. Everything exists as it is, and it comes and goes on its own accord. The last act of Truth is to make everything that has existed live in Heaven.

People live hidden by their life and body, karma and habit. What they know is based on their life; the environment where they grew up, what they learned at school, and what they did in society. Since people are deluded these false elements are them, they are blind and cannot see Truth.

One is Buddha and God when one is reborn as the true body and mind within nothingness. Then everything becomes Buddha and God, the oneness. People cannot understand the Bible and Sutras because their consciousness is bound to themselves. One whose consciousness lives in Truth is the whole, and therefore one can see and hear Truth.

To return to the perfect oneness is the great liberation. It is to have the great wisdom and to know that there is no sin and karma. The true world is where people become one with God and Buddha: the union of God and human.

Maum Meditation is returning to the originally existing God.

Maum Meditation Centers
Location And Contact Details

Please visit www.maum.org for a full list of addresses, phone and fax numbers, as well as the locations and contact details of over 220 South Korean regional centers.

[South Korea]
Nonsan Main Center
82-41-731-1114

[U.S.A.]
CA
Berkeley
1-510-526-5121
Campbell
1-408-508-9323
Irvine
1-949-502-5337
L.A. (Downtown)
1-213-484-9888
L.A. (Koreatown)
1-213-908-5151
Long Beach
1-562-912-7400
Orange
1-714-521-0325
San Diego
1-858-886-7363
San Fernando
Valley
1-818-831-9888
San Francisco
1-650-301-3012
Santa Clara
1-408-615-0435
West Covina
1-909-861-6888
CO
Denver
1-303-481-8844
FL
Miami
1-954-379-6394
GA
Atlanta (Suwanee)
1-678-698-8307

Smyrna
1-678-608-7271
HI
Honolulu
1-808-533-2875
IL
Chicago Loop
1-312-222-8989
Naperville
1-630-237-4166
North Brook
1-847-663-9776
MA
Boston
1-617-272-6358
MD
Ellicott City
1-410-730-6604
Rockville
1-301-770-7778
NC
Raleigh
1-919-771-3808
NJ
Palisades Park
1-201-592-9988
Teaneck
1-201-801-0011
NV
Las Vegas
1-702-254-5484
NY
Bayside
1-718-225-3472
Flushing
1-718-353-6678
Plainview
1-516-644-5231

PA
Elkins Park
1-215-782-8709
TX
Austin
1-512-585-6987
Dallas
1-469-522-1229
Fort Worth
1-817-581-6286
Houston
1-832-541-3523
Plano
1-972-599-1623
VA
Arlington
1-703-354-8071
Centreville
1-703-657-0550
WA
Federal Way
1-253-520-2080
Lynnwood
1-425-336-0754

[Argentina]
Almagro
54-11-4862-5691
Flores
54-11-4633-6598
Floresta
54-11-3533-7544

[Australia]
Perth (Mandurah)
61-8-9586-2070
Perth (Vic Park)
61-8-9355-4114
Sydney
61-2-9743-6427

[Bangladesh]
Dhaka
880-17-9544-8113

[Brazil]
Aclimacao
55-11-2537-5725
Brasilia
55-61-3877-7420
Sao Paulo
55-11-3326-0656

[Cambodia]
Phnom Penh
855-78-901-434

[Canada]
Mississauga
1-289-232-3776
Montreal
1-514-507-7659
Toronto
1-416-730-1949
Vancouver
1-604-516-0709

[Chile]
Santiago
56-2-2813-9657

[Colombia]
Batan
57-1-302-7832
Medellin
57-4-230-5001
Palermo
57-1-474-5202

[England]
London
44-208-715-1601

[France]
Paris
33-1-4766-2997

[Germany]
Berlin
49-30-2100-5344

[Guatemala]
Guatemala City
502-2360-6081

[Hong Kong]
852-2572-0107

[Hungary]
Budapest
36-1-950-9974

[India]
Gurgaon
91-97178-63915

[Indonesia]
Tangerang
62-21-5421-1699

[Italy]
Genova
39-349-364-2607
Milan
39-02-3940-0932

[Japan]
Kyoto
81-75-708-2302

Osaka
81-6-6777-7312
Saitama (Omiya)
81-48-729-5787
Sendai
81-22-762-9462
Tokyo (Machiya)
81-3-6806-6898
Tokyo (Shinjuku)
81-3-3356-1810
Yokohama
81-45-228-9926

[Kazakhstan]
Almaty
7-775-651-98-34

[Kenya]
Nairobi
254-789-154-445

[Laos]
Vientian
856-21-316-301

[Madagascar]
Antananarivo
261-34-91-203-08

[Malaysia]
Johor Bahru
60-7-361-4900
Kuala Lumpur
60-16-272-1081

[Mexico]
Mexico City
52-55-2614-7448
Tijuana
52-664-380-8109

[Myanmar]
Yangon
95-94-2113-9996

[New Zealand]
Auckland
64-9-480-7245
Christchurch
64-3-358-7247

[Panama]
507-399-4605

[Paraguay]
Asuncion
595-21-234-237

[Peru]
Lima
51-1-605-9425

[Philippines]
Clark
63-947-965-7462
Manila
63-2-687-1294

[Republic of
South Africa]
Pretoria
27-12-991-4986

[Russia]
Moscow
7-495-331-0660

[Singapore]
Marine Parade
65-6440-0323

Tanjong Pagar
65-6222-4171

[Sweden]
Stockholm
46-76-804-6806

[Taiwan]
Taipei
886-989-763-445

[Tanzania]
Dar es Salaam
255-76-3338-505

[Thailand]
Bangkok
66-2-118-3749

[Uganda]
Kampala
256-784-820-724

[Vietnam]
Hanoi
84-12-7365-8097
Ho Chi Minh City
84-8-5412-4989